11 RULES FOR LIFE

SECRETS TO LEVEL UP

Also by Chetan Bhagat

400 Days

The Girl in Room 105

One Arranged Murder

CHETAN BHAGAT

11 RULES FOR LIFE

SECRETS TO LEVEL UP

HARPER

NON-FICTION

An Imprint of HarperCollins *Publishers*

First published in India by Harper Non-fiction 2024
4th Floor, Tower A, Building No. 10, DLF Cyber City,
DLF Phase II, Gurugram, Haryana—122002
www.harpercollins.co.in

2 4 6 8 10 9 7 5 3 1

P-ISBN: 978-93-5699-997-8
E-ISBN: 978-93-5699-632-8

Typeset in 11.5/15.7 Warnock Pro at
Manipal Technologies Limited, Manipal

Printed and bound at
Nutech Print Services - India

This book is printed on FSC® certified paper
which ensures responsible forest management.

'You will amount to nothing.'

—My father

CONTENTS

Introduction   ix

The Zomato Delivery Guy and I   xiii

Pre-Rules Warm-Up: How the World
Actually Works   1

Rule #1: Never Ignore Your Fitness   16

Rule #2: Master Your Emotions   49

Rule #3: Put Yourself First   65

Rule #4: Master Simple English   76

Rule #5: No Cheap Dopamine   91

Rule #6: Chase the Hard Things   109

Rule #7: Eat the Elephant   118

Rule #8: Be the Cockroach   137

Rule #9: Learn to Connect with People   157

Rule #10: It's My Fault   174

Rule #11: Earn, Save and Invest   191

A Closing Note   208

Five Years Later   212

Acknowledgements   217

References   221

INTRODUCTION

I still remember that day in 2014. I was walking around Bandra, which is where I live in Mumbai. I passed Globus, a theatre that was screening *2 States*, a movie based on my book of the same name. The movie was a hit, the third one in a row after *3 Idiots* and *Kai Po Che!* Five thousand theatres around the country were screening the story that had once randomly popped up in my head. The country's biggest movie stars had worked for years, enacting characters I had created. Directors and other crew members had worked tirelessly to bring my story to life.

Continuing on my walk, I passed a bookshop. Many of my books were on the bestseller list; they had been there for years. It had been a decade since my first book had been published. The publishing industry, experts said, had never been the same again. My next book, *Half Girlfriend*, was also ready for release. Flipkart, a new online retailer at that time, had already booked the full front-page jacket of *The Times of India*, announcing my new book. The cost of the ad: a whopping two crore rupees! No book in India had ever had such an announcement.

I also wrote editorial columns on national issues in the same newspaper. I had brand endorsement deals, TV show offers and marketing tie-up opportunities—all unheard of for an author. In a country where one is lucky to sell a few thousand copies of a book, mine had sold millions. *Time* magazine had included me in the list of 'The 100 Most Influential People in the World'. Massive success had come my way, far beyond what I had ever imagined. I had had a tormented childhood and grew up in adverse circumstances in a country where few made it. Yet, as some would say, I had 'arrived'.

At that point, when my fame and success were at their peak, I was on a high. I didn't even fully realize how it had all happened. Today, ten years later, as the high has subsided, I have had a chance to reflect on my life. I have now lived for nearly five decades on this planet. That's a lot of life to study from. I have also had a chance to interact with many people who have 'made it' or 'arrived'. These include engineers, bankers, professors, movie stars, writers, media stalwarts, publishing industry heads, writers, politicians, CEOs, businessmen, start-up founders and billionaires. I have had a chance to study these successful people across different fields, as well as reflect on my own life. I have had time to observe and understand what works in life and what doesn't. This book is my way of giving back, my chance to share all that knowledge, wisdom and gyaan with you. This isn't just a quick motivational Instagram reel you swipe up and forget about. This is the distillation of everything I've learnt through my life.

Most people in India don't read any more. They are lost in their screens, watching mindless content day and night. The fact that you have picked up this book already puts you ahead of them. My only request would be to take what I say here seriously. (But don't be all serious and brooding in life—I can't imagine my readers like that!) This book has the power to transform your life IF you let it. Apply this knowledge. Take actual, concrete action after reading this book. Change something. I want you to do extremely well and be super happy. That's the only reason I have written this book. I have achieved enough, and I will keep doing more. But today, what gives me real joy is sharing my knowledge, using my writing skills and leveraging my popularity to reach you and help you get ahead. I want you to live an amazing life, become the best version of yourself, and reach your own massive success moment. I want you to be in the top echelons of society in terms of status. I want you to be one of the happiest people on earth.

It's not easy to achieve all this, but it's possible. I did it. You can as well. You just need to unlearn a few things and learn some new ones. You need to understand that life isn't about what they taught you in school. Nor is it what your well-meaning mom and dad told you at the dining table. The world isn't a nourishing, cuddly, loving place waiting to support you. No, that's the world your parents gave you as a child. As an adult, the real world is harsh and tough. India is more competitive than most other places in the world and hence it is even harder to make it here. It requires two things. One, a lot of work, and two, knowledge of some life secrets that nobody tells you in school, college or at home.

Let's make a deal. If you are ready to do the work, I will tell you these secrets. There are eleven in all.

Do we have a deal? Cool! Let's go!

Welcome to **11 Rules for Life**!

THE ZOMATO DELIVERY GUY AND I

My Zomato order was thirty minutes late. I checked the tiny bike icon on my app. My delivery partner, the guy bringing my order, was stuck around a kilometre away from my house. My little bowl of nourishment was with him. I called him, twice. His phone was busy. Gosh, I was hungry!

I told myself not to get worked up. It's only a delayed order of rajma–rice. I just had to sit on my couch and wait. Someone had cooked and packed my food. Someone else was carrying it in his backpack and riding a bike to bring it to me. A few thousand years ago, if I wanted food, I would have had to go out in the forest and brave wild animals. If I was lucky, I would find some fruit or hunt a little animal. No fruits or huntable animals on Bandra streets anymore. Now, apps did the hunting for me. My phone told me my order would be with me in a few minutes. All I had to do was relax and wait.

And yet I found it hard to relax. Images of steaming hot rajma–rice kept floating in my mind. Where is my food? Be here already, I screamed in my head. Hunger makes it difficult to feel grateful for modern technology or being better off than our hunter–gatherer ancestors.

My doorbell rang. I rushed to open the door. A dark-skinned man in his late twenties stood in front of me. He wore an ill-fitting red T-shirt, too tight around his chubby waist. The T-shirt had the Zomato logo. His face and hair were covered with sweat. He removed a huge black backpack to take out my food parcel. He was panting and trying to catch his breath.

'Sorry, I'm so sorry, sir,' he said, in a sincere, fearful and breathless voice. 'My bike broke down.'

I gave him a cursory nod. I took, almost snatched, the food from him as though I were an early man from the Stone Age who had found an apple after three days! I wondered if it would be rude to start eating right in front of him.

'Please don't leave me a bad review,' he said, joining his palms.

'What? No, I won't,' I said, 'but what happened? You were stuck at your location.'

'It … it was a bike puncture,' he said.

'Oh, how did you finally manage to here then?'

'I dragged the bike to the petrol pump, fixed the puncture and then drove. That is why the delay.'

'Really? But your location in the app didn't move at all.' I shot him an unconvinced look.

He remained quiet.

'I called you twice. Your phone was engaged. Are you sure your bike broke down?'

He looked at the floor, as if ashamed to give me the real answer.

'Anyway,' I said, 'I have my food, I'm good. No bad ratings or reviews needed.' I smiled at him.

'Thank you, sir!' He seemed visibly relieved. 'Sorry once again.'

'You want some water?' I asked.

He nodded. I went to the kitchen and returned with a glass of water. He stood staring at his phone, tears streaming down his face.

'Are you okay?' I said as I handed him the glass.

He nodded, composed himself and placed his phone back in his pocket. He took a sip of the water.

'What's your name?'

'Viraj. Viraj Shukla, sir. Why? You won't report me no, sir? Please don't, I will lose my job.'

'I won't. You seem upset. Just wanted to check if you are okay.'

'I'm okay.' He sighed. After a pause, he said, 'Actually I'm not okay, sir.'

He clenched his lips to prevent himself from crying again.

I checked the time. 2:30 p.m. I had a Zoom call with a client at 3 p.m.

'Do you have to make another delivery right now?' I said.

He shook his head.

'Lunch time is over. Deliveries are slow now until the evening,' he said.

'You want to tell me what happened?'

He looked at me, surprised and confused.

'What is making you so upset?' I opened the door a little further to allow him to enter.

'You are interested in my story, sir? Really?'

'Yeah. I have half an hour. I have to eat my lunch but ...'

'Please eat, sir. Please, I already made it late.'

'Have you had lunch?'

He shook his head.

'Fine, let's share.'

He looked dumbfounded but before he could refuse or say anything else, I gestured to him to come inside and quickly brought plates and cutlery from the kitchen.

I sat down at the dining table and opened the parcel of food.

'Come, Viraj, sit.'

'Sir, how can I have your food? And sit here with you?'

'Why? Bro, I want to listen to you. But I'm starving. And I can't just eat by myself with you talking to me. So please.'

I gestured to him to sit on the chair in front of me. Hesitantly, he sat down. I scooped out some rajma and rice onto his plate.

'Nobody has ever done this, sir,' Viraj said.

'It's fine. It's nice to have company.'

'Thank you,' he smiled.

'Let's eat. I'm famished.' I dug into my food, relishing the spoonfuls that landed in quick succession in my mouth.

We ate in silence for a minute before he spoke again. 'My bike did not break down, sir.'

'I know.'

'You do?'

'Yeah. You were on a call. That is what made you so disturbed. Right?'

'Yes, sir.'

'What happened?'

'My girlfriend broke up with me.'

'Oh,' I said, somewhat relieved. At least nobody had died.

'She was the love of my life. Meant everything to me.'

'Okay,' I said, spooning rice and rajma together, the current love of my life.

'Arpita and I had been together for the last eight years.'

'I understand. You were on a call with her?'

'Yes. She finally picked up after I had called her twenty times in the last week.'

'Twenty?'

'Maybe more. Thirty, forty. That's why it was now or never. My last chance to get her back.'

'And it didn't work, did it?'

He shook his head. He looked down at his plate. His eyes teared up again. He began to sob.

It's strange to see a fully grown, overweight man in a tight, bright red T-shirt, cry. I passed him a tissue.

'Sorry,' he said, composing himself again.

'Must have been some girl,' I said.

'I am a postgraduate, you know. I have an MA ... most delivery boys have not studied as much as I have.'

'Which subject?'

'History, sir.'

'Call me Chetan.'

'Okay, sir, I mean Chetan, sir.'

'How old are you, Viraj?'

'Twenty-nine.'

'Hmm ... and what do you want in life?'

'What life? My life is over. Arpita is gone. I have this job, which I could lose any time. Nothing I want from life. If I die tomorrow in a bike accident, it will be okay. Maybe that will be the best thing.'

I looked at him, stunned.

He gobbled down a few spoons of rajma–rice to quickly finish his meal.

'You want to die? At twenty-nine?' I said.

'What's the point of living, sir? You have no idea about my life. You have this beautiful house. You are a well-known writer. You have this wonderful life, with fame, money, respect. You obviously cannot understand why anyone would want their life to end. Your life is beautiful. Mine is terrible. So yes, death won't be a big loss, it will be a relief.'

'Don't talk like that.'

'It is true. I ride a bike twelve hours a day in heavy traffic. I pick up sandwiches and milkshakes from restaurants and take them to people's doors to satisfy their snack cravings. That's all I do. Yesterday, I drove forty minutes to deliver two paans. Can you believe it, Chetan sir? Driving 10 kilometres in rush hour to deliver two paans? The customer ate them in front of me. Gone in five seconds!'

I gave a wry smile. Paan would have been wonderful after rajma–rice, I thought. I scolded myself mentally and tried to focus on Viraj's words.

'Then I had to drive back again. To pick up another order an hour away. That's my life, day after day. My back hurts, my head hurts.'

'Why don't you take another job?'

'I will. But I needed a job urgently and this is all I could get.'

'Okay.'

'I had no money. Zero. This was a way to get some.'

'You do know there's nothing wrong in being a delivery boy, right?' I said. 'It's a respectable way to earn a living.'

'Yeah,' he said but looked unconvinced.

'The question though is this: Is that enough? For you?'

'Meaning?' Viraj looked blank.

'How much do you get paid?'

'Depends, say eighteen thousand a month on average.'

'Is that enough?'

'No. This is Mumbai. Just my rented room in a slum costs eight thousand rupees. Then there's food and other living expenses. I have nothing left at the end of the month.'

'Where are you from?'

'Yavatmal. It's in Maharashtra only.'

'I know the place. Is that where your parents stay?'

'Yes.'

'And your girlfriend too?'

'She did. But then she moved to Mumbai. To do an aviation academy course. I thought she had moved to this city for me. But ...' He fell silent mid-sentence.

'But what?'

'But she met another guy in Mumbai. And she left me for him. Threw away our eight-year-old relationship.'

'Threw away?'

'Fine, even I realize I didn't have a great career and couldn't promise a good future. That guy can do that.'

'Which guy?'

'Her new boyfriend. I have only seen him on her Instagram page once. She had posted a story in which she was sitting with him in his car.'

'Okay, he has a car.'

'Yeah. A BMW.'

'Do you have a car?'

'Why are you making fun of me, sir? Of course, I don't. How can I?'

'How can he?'

'He who?'

'The guy Arpita left you for.'

'I don't know, sir. Arpita said he works in a bank or something. He has a good salary.'

'And you don't.'

'No, sir.'

'And why is that?'

'Luck, sir. Everyone has their kismat.'

'Yeah? Everyone just *has* their kismat, is it? Do you think someone someday will call you and say, here, have some kismat?'

He looked up at me. To deflect my question, he adjusted his tight T-shirt.

'I need to get a bigger size,' he said, averting his eyes from mine.

I smiled.

'Yes, I know what you are thinking. I'm fat,' Viraj rubbed his neck as he spoke.

'I didn't say anything,' I said.

'Eighty-six kilograms. I'm five feet seven inches in height. I'm fat. I know it. All this happened over the last year.'

'It's okay. Is Arpita's new guy also as heavy?'

'No. He is slimmer. He's fit actually.'

'Why is that? Kismat?'

'I don't get time to exercise or cook healthy food, sir. Whatever I get at the end of the day, vada pav, samosas, I eat. I have no choice.'

I kept quiet.

'You have no idea how much I loved Arpita. That new guy can never love her that much.'

'And yet Arpita saw, which you say is correct too, a better future with him?'

'Girls are like that only.'

'Yeah? So, it's kismat's fault that you don't have a high-paying job, this job's fault that you can't eat healthy and the general nature of girls that you are now heartbroken?'

'Huh?' He looked shocked.

I checked my watch. My call was scheduled to start in five minutes.

'I need to go,' I said. 'Anyway, nothing is your fault, so nothing to be done. Nothing I say matters.'

'No, sir. Please continue. I think you are getting at something. I need to hear it.'

'I will say things that are hard for you to hear. They will hurt you or offend you. You will then blame me for making you feel worse about your life, which you already think is quite bad.'

'What hurt, offend? No, no. It's okay, please say it.'

'Not today. I must go,' I said and stood up. 'But let's do this. I will order lunch again tomorrow, after I finish my daily writing quota. Pick up that order around one o' clock. Would you be able to do that?'

'I can. If you tell me the exact time I will be waiting and ready to accept your order.'

'Cool, you bring me the food. I will tell you truths about life you need to hear. Done?'

'Done, sir. I will have to tell the other delivery boys in the area not to pick up the order from your address. Yes, done.'

'And no matter what, do not call or message Arpita anymore.'

'Huh? Okay, I won't. See you tomorrow,' he said and left.

⸻

'Perfect timing,' I said.

Viraj handed me my lunch parcel right on time. I took out the bowl of Sindhi curry that came with chapatis. I had ordered from a place called Sindhful, which specializes in Sindhi food. The runny, sour curry was a chef's special, made in a tomato base with various vegetables such as bhindi, baby corn and drumsticks. It looked and smelled delicious.

I offered to share my food with Viraj again but he refused.

'I ate already, a lot,' he said.

'Fine, I will also eat later then.' I kept my bowl aside.

'Tell me today's truth about life,' Viraj said.

'Sure. Did you call or message Arpita?'

'No. I wanted to, but I didn't. I promised you.'

'Did you see her Instagram posts?'

'Yes,' he said, avoiding my gaze. 'And I liked them too.'

'Oh dear.'

'I'm sorry. I miss her too much. She was my life.'

'Do you know why she was your life?'

'Because I love her?'

'No. Because apart from her you have no life. Sure, you are alive. But there was nothing good in your life apart from her. So her loss stings. A lot.'

'How can you say that, sir?'

'You disagree?'

'I don't know, sir. It just hurts. I don't know how my life became the way it is. I did everything right. I tried to, at least.'

'What right things did you do?'

'Followed what my parents told me to do. They encouraged me to work hard. Be a kind person. Respect others. Care for people. Basically, they said, be a good person and good things will happen to you. And that's what I tried to do.'

'And?'

'It didn't work. Look at my life. I have no money in the bank. Rather, I owe my friends forty thousand rupees. I have no girlfriend, no future.'

'You are only twenty-nine. How can you say you have no future?'

'Don't fool me, Chetan sir. I know I don't. I'm a delivery boy. People my age are software programmers, lawyers, CAs and doctors. I will never be that. This is my fate now.'

'Kismat?'

'Yes. You don't believe in it, but yes. It is luck. I studied like all the other students in school. Somehow, I got distracted in tenth standard and got low marks. Took Arts, then did graduation in History. People told me graduation isn't enough. I did my Masters. Then I came out of college and had no job. Searched for an entire year before becoming a delivery boy.'

'Okay, let's talk about that today.'

'What?'

'This doing the "right" thing. And kismat.'

'What about it?'

'That it's all nonsense. The way you think. Rather, the way you and millions of other young Indians have been made to think.'

'How do I think?'

'You don't think. You are only made to think.'

'By whom?'

'By those in society above you. Who want you to serve them.'

'I can think on my own.'

'No. You can't. Your brain has been lulled, hypnotized. Not just you. Millions like you. The underclass. The workers. The drones.'

'What?'

'I will tell you in detail. Ready for the lesson of the day?'

'Yes.'

'Good. Over the course of our next few meetings, I will be telling you my secret rules of life.'

'Secret rules? There are secret rules to life?'

'Yes. But before that, it is important to know how the world actually works.'

'Meaning?'

'Did they ever teach you how the world actually works in school or college?'

'No ... I mean ... I don't think so.'

'Exactly. Because they didn't want you to know. But now it is time for you to find out.'

PRE-RULES WARM-UP

HOW THE WORLD ACTUALLY WORKS

'No one is going to come help you. No one's coming to save you.'

—DAVID GOGGINS

The world we see first as a child is that of our home. When we are little, our home is the entire universe. We form our views on how people are and how they behave based on what happens in our immediate family. However, we do not realize that as children, we get an extra level of attention and caring than what exists in the world. When you were hungry, all you had to do was cry. Your mother brought you food. She would feed you, clean you, and give you kisses and hugs just for finishing your lunch. When you learnt to walk or talk, everyone home became excited and cheered for you. You felt loved and supported. All this made you believe the world outside is the same.

When you started school, your early years too were about the same love and support. There were numbers and nursery rhymes to learn, fun games to play, and hardly any pressure. You sang at assembly and your teachers told you stories in class. They also taught you moral values—of being good, honest, fair and kind.

As you grew older, you learnt more new things. You were taught that those who work hard get rewarded in life. You learnt about equality and justice. Or how everyone born on this earth must have equal rights and opportunities. Studies became harder as school progressed. However, when you did well, everyone praised you. If you topped the class or won a race on sports day, you received a medal. Hence, you learnt the concept of meritocracy. You do well, people will applaud you, support you and give you an award. Nobody is out to get you. The world just wants you to progress and rise.

Sorry, but all this is not true. Sure, people want all these good values to exist. Many even believe they exist. They see the world like Exhibit I below. It is like seeing the world from the top. It appears flat. There are people, and they all exist in society, with equality, fairness and justice. Hence, work hard, get good marks and you will be rewarded, loved and supported.

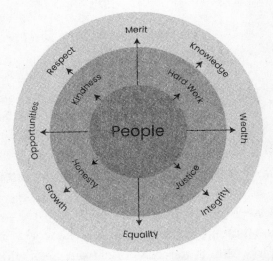

EXHIBIT I: *THE FLAT, EVERYTHING-IS-EQUAL, PEOPLE-ARE-GOOD-AND-FAIR, TOP VIEW OF THE WORLD*

However, it is a distorted, false view of the world compared to how things actually are. The reality is that the world is not flat when it comes to how society is organized. Instead of the flat top view, it is better to see the world from an overall perspective and realize that it is more like a 3D mountain. The everything-is-fair-and-equal flat-view model of the earth ignores something big—class and hierarchy. The world is a mountain made of several tiers. For clarity, I will simplify them into three main tiers. Imagine the world to be like a three-tiered mountain, like a wedding cake. This is represented in Exhibit II.

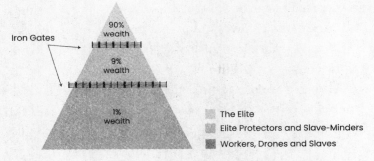

EXHIBIT II: *THE THREE-CLASS MODEL OF THE WORLD*

Look at Exhibit II carefully. This is how the world is organized (but nobody tells you that). The world classifies its people within a hierarchy of classes. Let's talk about each of them in some detail.

Class I: The Elite

At the top is the Elite class or Class I—the rich, powerful and famous, or a combination of all three. These are industrialists, entrepreneurs, politicians, media moguls, movie producers, movie directors, movie stars, sportspeople, fund managers, investors, CEOs, CFOs and people at the absolute top of their fields. They are the smallest class in terms of number of people, commonly referred to as the '1 percenters' in popular media, implying they are only around 1 per cent of the world's population. I don't have exact percentages and this 1 per cent is just an educated estimate. However, they wield the most clout, and control almost everything that happens in this world.

I'm not being a conspiracy theorist. I'm not implying that the 1 per cent Elite talk to each other and plan to screw over the rest of the world. That's not true. This 1 per cent of the world's 8 billion population, that is 80 million, is still a large number. These 80 million people can't all be connected or conspiring against the rest. However, these 1 percenters collectively control most of the world's resources, money and power. Like any other human being, they make decisions based on what is best for them. Hence, invariably, they use all that the world has to offer to serve themselves first. Sure, they want to sound and look good. Some of them talk of helping the world or of equality. But they are obviously quite happy with the unequal place they have in society, which is in the top 1 per cent. People don't find inequality unjust when they are the ones with the unfair advantage.

I'm not judging these people. Some would say, and rightly so, that I too belong to this class now. However, I was one of you at one point. I want you to get here as well. My purpose of writing this book is to help you join this elite 1 per cent class. It's hard as hell if you don't already belong there, but it isn't impossible. It is difficult because heavy Iron Gates that act as entry barriers block those below from reaching the peak of the mountain. The Elite are not only protected by these Iron Gates but also by a whole other class which guards and protects the Elite. This is what I call Class II, the Protectors.

Class II: Elite Servers, Protectors and Slave-Minders

Class II, or the second class of people are those who serve, protect and work for the Elite. They are around 9 per cent of the total population (again, I don't have an exact percentage, so this is just my rough estimate). Class II is still a minority but is a lot larger than the elite 1 percenters. Class II Elite Protectors are the white-collared class, the lawyers, doctors, engineers, bankers, accountants, certain higher grade government employees, sales managers, executives working in MNCs and similar level professions. They are the upper-middle class, who, if they save like hell, could also become borderline Class I-level rich. They are the bourgeois of the French Revolution, the people who are fewer in numbers, are not the super elite but still have significant influence. The Elite hire them to run their corporations and factories, get their hospital treatments, do their accounts, and serve them in other ways. Elite Protectors also perform another essential function. They manage the class below them, or Class III—the workers, drones and slaves. The Class III population is the largest in this world, and easily outnumbers the other two classes above it. If this class is not managed well, it could shake the world. It could take back control from the Elite (indeed, that is what happened in some socio-economic revolutions in the history of our world). However, for the most part, Class II ensures that Class III behaves itself well. Class III plays its role of being workers, drones and slaves for the world, and the Elite Protector Class ensures this hierarchical way of functioning continues to run in a smooth manner. The inter-class Iron Gates prevent 'class jumps', or climbing up to a higher class. The Class II Elite Protectors further ensure class jumps are rare, especially from Class III to an upward class. For instance, some Elite Protectors work for a multinational corporation in management roles. When hiring new people, they see to it that they hire from the same Elite Protector Class. They only recruit from the colleges where the children of Elite Protectors study. They almost never allow a Class III drone to join them at their level. Their instinctive nature is to not allow anybody below them to rise easily.

Class III: Drones, Workers and Slaves

This is society's largest segment, at probably around 90 per cent of the population. In India especially, the existence of this underclass is stark and obvious. Income levels are lower and vary significantly even within this class. This segment comprises the poor, lower-middle class and middle class. Money is always tight for people in this category. The highest anyone in this class normally aspires to reach is the middle class. The middle-class level in India, a relatively low per capita income country, isn't a particularly high standard of living anyway.

Class III people do most of the work to run our country. People in this category start from the lowest-paying jobs—daily labourers, domestic helpers, janitors, workers at roadside stalls, etc. This category also includes clerks, delivery boys, retail salespeople you see in shops at malls, waiters, hotel staff, factory workers, drivers, cooks, receptionists, cleaners, the person who comes to connect your Wi-Fi at home, the guy at the mobile phone repair shop, and similar professions. People in this class make just about enough for them to survive. If there is an emergency spend like say an unexpected, big medical expense, the Class III person ends up in debt. Even if Class IIIs try their best to save money, they never accumulate reasonable wealth or assets. They cannot afford expensive education for their children. As a result, they stay in this class all their life, as do their kids. The Iron Gates, which we will discuss in the next section, are extra strong here to prevent Class IIIs from moving up.

The Iron Gates

What keeps this class hierarchy intact are the Iron Gates. These are the various entry barriers, which make it almost impossible for someone to jump class. Sure, sometimes class jumps do happen in India. When it does, it is seen as a rare event. Those who have done so become mini heroes. However, most people are expected to remain in their class and never attempt to break open the Iron Gates. Exhibit III shows what comprises the Iron Gates, or the actual reasons why class jumping is so hard.

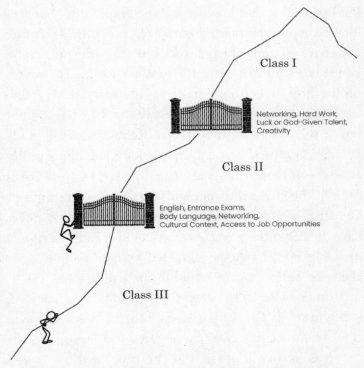

Class I

Networking, Hard Work,
Luck or God-Given Talent,
Creativity

Class II

English, Entrance Exams,
Body Language, Networking,
Cultural Context, Access to Job Opportunities

Class III

EXHIBIT III: *THE IRON GATES - CHALLENGES THAT PREVENT JUMPING CLASS*

For instance, one key barrier to jumping from Class III to Class II is English. Without good English-speaking skills, you are judged and condemned to remain in Class III in India. Of course, if you are already in Class I, this won't apply. A powerful politician or successful sportsman fluent in Hindi but poor in English will not be judged as much. English is just one of the locks at the Iron Gates that prevent a class jump. Other barriers include hyper-competitive entrance exams. These require a massive amount of hard work but may offer successful candidates an opportunity to class jump. However, only a tiny percentage make it. The rest are rejected, depleted of the energy and resources they have spent trying to clear these monstrous exams. Similarly, body language, cultural context, networking, job opportunity access—all these things are usually used as Iron Gates to keep the lower class out and away from better jobs or opportunities. For instance, a delivery boy would never have the networking needed to get a job at a multinational firm. His body language alone will remind people of his class and automatically limit his opportunities.

Iron Gates exist between Class II and Class I as well. A big jump to Class I is reserved for the very few who can break or climb over these gates and jump up. This requires networking right at the top, hard work well beyond the average, a certain amount of luck or god-given talent and creativity. Mostly, Class I people like to keep this extremely rare '1 percenter' class to themselves and for their kids, who automatically become the next generation Class I.

Your Goal: To Cross Your Aukaat and Jump Class

You have no control over where you are born—in Class I, II or III. Moreover, society is designed to keep you in that same class throughout your life. Most people are so caught up with basic survival that the barriers seem insurmountable and that makes them accept their fate.

However, in recent times, technology has changed a few things. Today, no matter which class you belong to, you can see on social media how people of the higher classes live their lives. You know exactly where the country's rich, famous and influential go on vacation, which cars they drive, the food they eat and the houses they live in. For most people, this is fun to watch. It is voyeuristic entertainment and a way of living vicariously. Most people know they will never go to London for a holiday or drive a Mercedes Benz SUV. However, it's fun to see their favourite movie star living that life. Between making food deliveries of biryani, a delivery boy can see the Maldives resort where his favourite actress went. An accounts intern on a Mumbai local can see the Austrian spa where her favourite actor goes to get in shape. That's all the accounts intern will ever hope for in life, to watch these images of the wonderful life even as she scrambles

> If you believe in stuff like equality, equal opportunities and "good things happen to good people", you have been fooled. You are born into a class. You are expected to remain in your area of the class mountain. Try to climb up, and you will stumble against the Iron Gates.

to survive and serve the higher classes.

And that is how the world actually works. If you believe in stuff like equality, equal opportunities and 'good things happen to good people', you have been fooled. You are born into a class. You are expected to remain in your area of the class mountain. Try to climb up, and you will stumble against the Iron Gates. You will also be kicked back down. It's not fair. In fact, it's highly unfair. It's not supportive. It's rigged.

However, now that you know this, you can do something about it. Your eyes are open. You have seen the mountain in 3D, as a whole, rather than a distorted, fake, flat view from the top. Now, you can find a path amongst the rocks, cracks and jagged edges to slowly climb up while nobody is looking. You can smash open the Iron Gates and jump across the barriers. Your life's mission can be to climb up the class mountain until you reach the top.

There's a concept in India called *aukaat*, a word which has no exact English translation, but 'status' comes somewhat close. To achieve success is to jump class and cross your aukaat. You too can cross your aukaat and advance to levels that are unexpected, perhaps even unimaginable, even for you. You may or may not finally reach the absolute top. But adopting this mindset of crossing your aukaat will ensure one thing—you will reach your potential and become the best version of yourself. You will get to a better place, even if not the best place. You will live a more worthwhile life.

All this is a quest to fight the sharks and cross the seas to reach greener, calmer shores. It's tough. However, it's a hell of a lot better than wasting your life. There's pain in progress, but there's pain in stagnation and decline too. It's hard to do well, but it's equally hard to live a life of failure. Choose your pain and choose your hard.

If progress is what you choose, congratulations! You are with me. I will now prepare you to fight this tough battle, win and be rewarded for it. I will tell you how to get a life filled with success, joy and happiness. In the coming chapters, I will give you my eleven secret rules of success and life. You must follow them if you want to win. Nobody will tell you these secrets. For nobody really cares about you. I do, which is why I wrote this book. Read, understand and implement these rules in your life with full attention and devotion.

Do not see this book as yet another piece of content—a

> There's pain in progress, but there's pain in stagnation and decline too. It's hard to do well, but it's equally hard to live a life of failure. Choose your pain and choose your hard.

mindless Insta reel, an inspirational YouTube video, a quote you read on a poster. All those things take minutes to make. This book has required me to live five decades of my life to write. So if you want a TL; DR version, a quick summary, or just the headlines because 'you don't have time' or 'you are not really a reader', then STOP. Just stop right here. Leave, and go back to your mediocre, instant-gratification life. If you don't realize that important things in life require focus, attention and deep work, how are you ever going to make it? I can transform your life. Give you something that nobody will ever give you. All I need from you is your focus and commitment. Do I have it?

....

Key Takeaways

- The atmosphere you grow up in at home, school and college is entirely different from that of the outside world.

- Accept that a world based on merit, equality, hard work, truth and fair play doesn't exist. This is your first step to moving ahead in life.

- The world functions on the concept of class and hierarchy, and moving from one class to another is extremely difficult.

- An unfair world doesn't feel unfair to the one with all the advantages.
- Breaking class barriers requires a lot of painful, hard work. Which pain would you rather choose—stagnating and being unhappy, or the one you need to endure to move ahead?

....

'You have my focus,' Viraj said, 'and I will commit one hundred per cent.'

'Good, what do you want?'

'I want to jump class. I am Class III. My father too. He was a factory worker. As was my grandfather.'

'You can jump. Are you ready to do the work for it?'

'I can try. Tell me what to do. Where to start?'

'I will tell you. But you will have to get me my lunch again tomorrow.'

I walked Viraj to the door.

'But—'

Before Viraj could say any more, I added with a smile, 'Chinese tomorrow. Is Royal China good? Will order from there,' and waved him goodbye.

He waved back, still looking perplexed.

RULE #1

NEVER IGNORE YOUR FITNESS

'Physical fitness is not only one of the most important keys to a healthy body, it is the basis of dynamic and creative intellectual activity.'

—JOHN F. KENNEDY

Whatever you want to do in life, fitness always comes first.

Fitness, while seen as a good thing to possess, is not usually the first item on a list of to-dos for a successful life or career. You will probably wonder, what's the point of building biceps when I'm preparing for IIT-JEE? Why should I build cardiovascular strength if I'm trying to get a decent job? Why is this advice here?

I'm guilty of thinking like this in the past. I know now that it is the wrong way to think. The first rule, by a big margin, for a happy and successful life is to always pay attention to your health and fitness. Read on.

My Mistakes with Fitness

I was always the fat kid. 'Roly-poly', 'chubby', 'healthy' (in a bad, Punjabi-usage way) and 'fat' were the terms used to describe me as a child. I didn't realize it then, but somewhere it altered my personality. The 'fat kid' classification had an impact on my confidence. Not only did I feel underconfident about my looks, but I also felt underconfident about myself. In school, I kept away from sports, even as I envied my classmates who played basketball and cricket.

Somehow, I had accepted my fate—some kids are just fat and I'm one of them, I told myself. I didn't ever think it was in my control, and that I could exercise and watch what I ate to fix the problem.

I also saw food as one of the big joys of life. I grew up in a household where there was constant conflict, especially between my mother and father. My father was exceptionally strict with me. Also, something I haven't really talked about before is that my neighbour, an older boy, used to molest me. In this messed-up situation, food, especially the tasty, unhealthy kind, was one of the few things that made me feel good. From chole–bhature and rasgullas to halwa, malai–chini toast and condensed milk on bread—I would eat whatever I could find. I convinced myself I was not meant to be athletic or one of those sporty kids. I would study. If at all I participated in extracurriculars, it would not involve any physical activity. Perhaps that is why I took to writing!

This attitude continued through college and into my work life when I was in a bank abroad. In every picture with friends or colleagues, I used to be the one who was most overweight. I still didn't do much about it. It took me a long time to realize my mistake. The lack of fitness had played havoc with my body, mental state and happiness. Sure, I had many other things going right for me. However, I could never enjoy life as much as I should have. Nor could I reap the various mental benefits fitness provides, which may have helped me achieve much more in life.

Today, I prioritize fitness over everything else. I haven't missed a workout in five years. I run, I lift, I try to eat well, take care of my sleep and control stress.

Everything can wait—fitness cannot. I'm not perfect. I still slip, particularly on my diet—forty-five years of indiscipline is not that easy to wipe out. But I'm striving to get better. Every day, one step at a time. And I assure you, you can too.

Why Fitness?

People pursue fitness for several reasons. The three main ones are: aesthetics, physical strength and mental strength. Let's look at each of these below.

Fitness for Aesthetics

A big reason for people to start on a fitness journey is to look good. Most people want to get a hot six-pack or look slim in pictures.

It's a perfectly valid goal, though this isn't why fitness is the number one secret rule of life for me. Sure, looks matter in life. No matter what you do, if you are good-looking, life gets easier. There are obvious professions where looks are extremely important, such as modelling, acting, and so forth. However, in the real world, a handsome accountant or a beautiful lawyer will also have certain advantages over their peers at work. Is it fair? No. The quality of one's work should be the only basis of judging people in an office, isn't it? But an office is full of human beings and human beings aren't fair. A good-looking or attractive person, by definition, draws more attention. In all likelihood, it also encourages people to judge them more favourably. Whether you are at a job interview, making a point in a work meeting, making a sales pitch, or raising money for your business—better looks help. They get you those few extra seconds of attention and a positive response from the listener, which you can then use to sell yourself or your ideas.

Sure, without substance, just looks won't help beyond a point. But assuming you do have the substance in place, good looks are a great advantage to have.

You cannot change certain aspects about your physicality—your features, height, hair, etc. But you can, in most cases, control your weight. You can also become muscular and toned, which is a great enhancer of looks. If you are a short, bald and fat man instead of a short, bald and fit man—there is a big difference in how people will see you. If you are a girl, being fit is one of the best ways to enhance your looks. Hence, aesthetics or looks is a good enough reason to pursue fitness. However, the two reasons that follow are even more important.

Fitness for Physical Strength

Becoming fit also means becoming stronger and having more endurance and power. There are other aspects such as balance, flexibility and agility as well. Today, we don't need raw strength as much as humans did tens of thousands of years ago. Back then, humans had to climb trees to pick fruits. They had to chase and fight animals to hunt them. They had to build houses and collect hay to keep themselves warm. Today, we have remotes and touchscreens, with which we can execute nearly any task with almost no effort.

This doesn't mean we don't need physical strength in present times. We still need a certain amount to go about our day, and not be absolutely exhausted at the end of it.

We need stamina to sit and study for long periods of time. We need to travel from place to place to meet clients or close business deals. We need to maintain our homes, ourselves and our families—all of which require physical stamina and strength. Without some degree of physical strength, the battle to make a class jump also becomes more difficult.

Can you stay up all night to study for an entrance exam, or does your body collapse under the stress? Can you visit ten stores across various parts of the city to sell your product, come home and reply to two dozen emails and answer ten phone calls? Can you do all this and still have time to be with your family and play with your kids? That is what it takes to survive and win in life. If each day ends in massive exhaustion, how are you going to live your best life? Fitness is vital for physical strength and endurance. Greater physical strength and endurance not only boost your immunity but also reduce your risk of health complications such as cardiac issues, diabetes and hypertension.

Fitness for Mental Strength

The mental benefits of being fit make it the first secret rule for success. Innumerable scientific studies now show that exercise leads to mental well-being and lowers stress and anxiety. Added to that is the fact that a fitness routine also toughens you up to face the world.

> Exercise requires motivation, focus and discipline. It demands pushing aside that inner voice making excuses or asking you to quit. This is exactly what success in life requires as well.

Fitness is hard. The world is hard. Fitness comprises exercise and diet. Exercise requires motivation, focus and discipline. It demands pushing aside that inner voice making excuses or asking you to quit. This is exactly what success in life requires as well. Every time you go to the gym or go for a run, you're basically doing net-practice sessions for the world. Treat the aesthetic and physical strength benefits as by-products.

Hard exercise teaches you to control your mind. It tells you to keep going when you don't want to. Bodybuilders with decades of fitness experience say that on most days they don't feel like going to the gym. However, they have trained themselves to ignore that quitter, loser, excuse-maker voice inside them. You will constantly battle with this loser inner voice throughout your life. This voice will tell you to choose the easy way out. It will direct you towards instant gratification. It will encourage you to be lazy, eat unhealthy, drink alcohol, watch TV non-stop and spend hours on Insta reels. You have to become good at telling this voice to shut the hell up. Exercise is great practice to learn how to silence your loser voice.

The second part of fitness is controlling your diet, which also teaches you many life lessons. To diet properly, you need non-stop discipline. Planning a healthy diet requires you to pay attention to what you eat 24/7. This is unlike exercise, for which you need to push yourself for about an hour in the gym. Maintaining a good diet will also require you to give up temptation. You have to resist and say no to that pack of biscuits in the kitchen, the mithai box left over from Diwali, ice-cream at a party, or a plate of French fries in a restaurant. The more you practice restraint, the better you get at self-control in other aspects of your life. A good diet also requires massive patience. You don't become fit if you eat well for only one day. It takes months, sometimes years of work with no daily results to speak of.

Discipline, resisting temptation, patience—all these qualities help you in life as well. Fitness isn't just a way for you to be in shape and look good. It is a life laboratory. It will help you build the ability to endure pain and give up pleasure, which is a phenomenal power in life. Society will constantly toss cheap pleasures at you—video games, TV, OTT content, fast food and social media. Most people are soft and weak. They will get sucked into these pleasures. But if you become strong—not only physically but also mentally—you will choose the necessary pain over pleasure. Eventually, you will win, in the gym and in life. Hence, it all begins with fitness.

A Good, Practical Fitness Routine

I am no fitness expert. I am a fitness student. There are tons of online resources that you can access if you want to get started on a fitness plan. They have been created by experts who do it for a living. YouTube channels such as Athlean-X or The Buff Dudes, for example, have wonderful videos on diet and fitness. There are fitness content creators like Alexia Clark on Instagram. Some Indian YouTube channels include The Body Workouts, The Shilpa Shetty Kundra, and Mind With Muscle. A lot of the content on these channels is free, and I recommend you spend some time going through them to figure out which one will suit you best, as each individual is different.

Here, I can guide you in a real, practical way. I can tell you what works for me, someone who was never fit throughout my life.

What I have found is that people don't lack information about how to achieve their fitness goals. However, it is their mindset which prevents them from breaking bad habits. It is only when people realize how being fit flows into every realm of success and happiness and that it is indeed the number one thing to focus on in life, that they make a real change. Hopefully, what you read above has somewhat helped you change the way you see fitness.

A Basic Fitness Plan (For People Like Me Who Never Took Fitness Seriously)

Keep It Simple

The simpler your plan, the more likely you are to stick to it. This applies to life in general, as well as to fitness. While my plan is universal and basic, I realize every individual is different, as is the starting point of every fitness journey. You could be really overweight right now, in which case your first priority will be to lose some weight. Or, even though you may not be fat, you may feel weak or less energetic, and therefore you need more strength and stamina. Feel free to tweak the plan below as per your requirements. I also recommend you consult a doctor before you incorporate any new diet or exercise regimen in your life.

The Three Pillars of Fitness

Fitness is composed of three pillars. These are sleep, diet and exercise. For each pillar, you need a simple, effective system.

The first one is extremely important (and is the least discussed), so let's start with it.

1. Sleep[1]

Multiple scientific studies show the direct impact of sleep on our happiness and energy levels in our life. We feel and function better if we sleep better. Good quality sleep for a sufficient duration, which is around seven to eight hours for most people, is a must if you are chasing success and happiness in life. A new day

> A new day doesn't begin when you wake up, it begins when you go to bed the night before.

doesn't begin when you wake up, it begins when you go to bed the night before. The first step to having a great day is getting sound sleep for the requisite hours the previous night. Studies show that during a full night of sleep, we make our emotional and physical recovery. That is why, if you haven't slept enough or restfully at night, the next day either your head hurts or your body hurts or you feel light-headed and weak. Along with recovery, other subconscious processes such as hormone regulation occur during sleep. If you don't get enough rest, it will lead to hormonal imbalance and make you perform sub-optimally. Your concentration and focus for studies, your gains in the gym and your creativity will be affected by the lack of good sleep. So here are some ways to ensure good sleep quality:

Your Fitness Plan—Sleep

1. **Sleep on Time and at Roughly the Same Time Every Day:** If you read up reliable material on the science of sleep, you will find that our bodies have evolved to the circadian rhythm, or Earth's natural

cycle of day and night. When it gets dark, certain hormones are activated in our brain that make us less alert, more relaxed and eventually make us feel sleepy. In an ideal world, we should sleep soon after dark. However, it's not practical to do so in modern life. For those with regular working hours, setting a sleep time between 10 p.m. to 11 p.m. is a good system. But you can set whatever time works best for you. Note that a set sleep time means being in bed with the lights out (and with phones and other devices kept out of reach) by that time.

2. **Don't Look at Bright Screens before You Sleep:** Many of us (yes, I'm guilty of this too) scroll through our phones right before we go to bed. Bright light at night confuses our brain's circuitry, triggering the release of daytime hormones and neurochemicals. These include neurochemicals that make us feel more alert, making it difficult to sleep. Some of the content we watch at night on social media could be disturbing as well. This can cause a clutter of thoughts and anxiety in our head and lead to overthinking—all undesirable things before going to bed. So keep away from that screen and charge your phone in a different room at night if you can.

3. **Ensure Your Room Is Dark, Quiet and Cool:** Studies show that darkness and optimum temperatures co-relate to a better night's sleep. Blackout curtains,

cardboard sheets or whatever it takes to make your room dark will help. If that is not possible, get hold of a comfortable eye mask. Similarly, cut noise levels or get good earplugs. If you have air-conditioning, set the temperature a few degrees lower than you do in the day (though you have to ensure it doesn't become uncomfortably cold either). These little steps can go a long way in preparing you for a good sleep.

4. **Don't Drink Alcohol or Caffeine before Bed:** Both these substances affect the quality of sleep, although in different ways. Caffeine is a stimulant, which blocks sleep-inducing chemicals from reaching their receptors. This is why the world is addicted to tea and coffee. Caffeine makes us alert and energetic, even if for a while, which may be helpful in the daytime. I, for one, love coffee and the perk-up it provides. However, you don't need such stimulation at night. A good thumb rule is to stop consuming caffeine post 2 p.m., though different people have different levels of tolerance. Alcohol too has a detrimental effect on your sleep. Studies show that while alcohol may make people feel sleepy, the quality of sleep one gets after consuming alcohol is poor. One doesn't get deep REM (Rapid Eye Movement) sleep, the phase during which the maximum rest and recovery happens for us. Ideally, one should not consume alcohol at all, because of its many other harmful effects apart from

poor sleep. If one does consume it, it should be on rare occasions, in limited quantity and several hours before one's sleep time. Avoid having more than two drinks in one evening, and overall, no more than seven drinks a week. Many of us attend parties that carry on late into the night and involve excessive alcohol consumption. You may think you are having fun or bonding with friends, but regular consumption of alcohol could lead to addiction, liver damage and many other problems, including hurting your sleep cycle. Cut out alcohol completely or reduce its intake as much as you can.

5. **Cut Stress from Your Life:** This is easy to say, but hard to implement. Stress reduction often requires making considerable changes to your life. When you are working hard to make those class jumps, there will be stress. There is also stress in daily commutes, family obligations, relationship expectations and your work life. Anxiety comes from uncertainty about the future. Studies show that while stress in moderate doses help us focus, too much stress has detrimental effects. Stress leads to the release of the hormone cortisol, which impacts sleep quality. You can't eliminate stress completely, but you must aim to lessen it. Only keep the stress that arises from things most important to you and let go of everything else. If work and family are your focus, ignore all

the other nonsense—what others say about you, and what people expect from you, for instance. We stress too much about things that don't really matter to us. Similarly, try to cut work commutes or other routine stressors to the extent you can. I would rather live in an apartment

❝You can't eliminate stress completely, but you must aim to lessen it. Only keep the stress that arises from things most important to you and let go of everything else.❞

half the size but walking distance to work than far away in a bigger house. A peaceful life is far more valuable than a few hundred extra square feet.

6. **Wake Up on Time, Around the Same Time, and Get Some Sunshine:** If you sleep around the same time every day, chances are you will start waking up around the same time every day as well. Maintain this, even on weekends. Your body works best when it matches the daily rhythm of the earth. This isn't just a poetic concept; it is scientifically tested. It is an amazing self-regulating system designed by nature, which makes us active during the day and relaxed at night. Sadly, humans have created this modern life which has led to the disruption of this beautiful sleep and wakefulness cycle. Once you wake up, don't use your phone at all in the first hour. (Okay, I know that sounds like punishment. Fine, no phone for half an

hour after you wake up!) Get some sunlight, ideally not through a window. Be exposed to daylight, even though you don't have to be directly under the sun. The morning sun rays help release hormones and neurotransmitters in your body, which make you alert and energetic throughout the day.

2. Diet

Once you sort out your sleep, it is time to attack the second and (at least for me) toughest pillar of fitness—diet. You have heard the cliché: 'You are what you eat.' A balanced, nutritious diet is easy on paper. You know what you must do—eat less, eat healthy. You understand that vegetables, fibre, protein should be the bulk of your diet. You are aware that you must limit fat and sugar. And yet, after a day's work, when you are tired and hungry, and then see a spread of hot samosas, chips, mithai and chaat, all this knowledge goes for a toss.

There's something about food. At least for some of us (like me), food is fun, pleasure, warmth, comfort and joy all rolled into one. This is not a great way to think. Food is meant to be fuel. For early humans, food was hard to find, requiring hours of foraging in the jungle and facing the risk of being attacked by a wild animal while trying to find an evening snack. Today, humans have altered all that. Food is now available easily and relatively cheaply.

Multinational companies sell and market food designed to tickle your taste buds and give you a rush of sugar. You don't need to hide from a pack of wolves to find an apple to eat in the forest. You simply open the refrigerator and take out a tub of ice-cream.

Clearly, our bodies are not designed for this hyper-convenient world of super-flavoured foods. Fatty and sugary foods evoke an evolutionary response. In prehistoric days, chancing upon an item with high sugar content was equivalent to hitting the jackpot. Since both sugar and fat give much-needed energy to the body, humans would rush to eat it as they knew they may not get food the next day. Today, a plate of samosas and gulab jamun evokes the same primitive response even though there is no scarcity of food around you. None of the readers of this book, I can bet, will ever have to fear starving to death. Yet, we can't seem to control our evolutionary response and end up messing up our diets all the time.

This is the core issue behind every failed diet plan. *You and I will never be able to fully overcome the temptation to eat unhealthy food.* Unhealthy foods are designed that way. What you can do is, with practice, find a balance in your life. Aim to mostly eat healthy, but also let go a bit sometimes. However, ensure that you only let go *'a bit'*. Such are the consequences of eating the highly processed junk foods of today that one cheat meal can screw up a week of good dieting. Enjoy occasional, moderate treats but commit to living a life of largely healthy eating, comprising real, natural, whole foods.

Eventually, you will start enjoying healthy food and crave less of the unhealthy stuff. Your mindset will shift and food will become what it is supposed to be—fuel for your body and mind.

The box below gives you some options for a diet plan. You can find many more online and should also consider consulting a doctor.

Fitness Plan—Diet

1. **Count Your Calories:** Diet is simple arithmetic. Calories in minus calories out will tell you if you are gaining or losing weight. To lose weight, aim to eat 300 to 500 calories less per day than you burn. This is a fine calculation and requires some precision. Calorie-counting tools can help at the start before you learn to intuitively regulate yourself. I recommend the MyFitnessPal app, which is a meal and activity tracker. There are others such as HealthifyMe as well. You set up your profile, add your goals and the MyFitnessPal app will tell you how much you can eat every day. It also has a database of every food item imaginable (including Indian food). You simply add foods as you eat them. If you use

it honestly, MyFitnessPal works quite wonderfully. Track what you eat on the app for thirty days. See if you can take it to ninety days. Continue as needed until you reach your weight goal.

2. **Intermittent Fasting (IF):** Intermittent Fasting refers to not consuming any calories at all for a set period of hours in a twenty-four-hour day. Some say IF is just a fancy term to describe skipping breakfast. They are not wrong. The most common IF duration is sixteen hours, done from dinner the night before until lunch the next day (hence the skipping of breakfast). If you finish dinner by 8 p.m., and don't eat anything until 12 noon the next day, you have fasted for sixteen hours. This fasting results in many benefits such as increasing your metabolism and your body's ability to use existing fat stores. IF also mimics our evolutionary past, where food was not always available. Hence, humans went through periods of hunger on a regular basis. When you do IF, you get intensely hungry near the end of your fasting window. This is normal. Overall, IF has one main benefit—it makes dieting simple. It makes it clear what to eat in that sixteen-hour window—which is not nothing (you are allowed black tea, black coffee, soda water, diet drinks, etc.). In the remaining window of eight hours, you can eat as per your calorific quota, which you would have determined through your fitness app.

To be clear, *calorie counts are important despite IF.* Many people mistakenly believe that if they do IF, they can eat whatever they want in those eight hours. That is incorrect. You eat your daily calorie quota—or a small deficit if you want to lose weight. You consume food in the eight-hour window, in two meals or in two meals and a small snack. Given you have your entire daily quota of calories to eat in those eight hours, you can normally have two decent-sized meals. Intermittent fasting works well for me. It is sometimes difficult to stay hungry until lunch. On some days, I relax the sixteen-hour rule. For instance, it is okay to do it for fourteen hours sometimes (say the days I'm staying in a nice hotel with a fabulous free breakfast buffet and I know I am not missing that!). If I'm sensible about total calories, IF will show results. Try it. Keep at it for twenty-one days, and then see if you can maintain this for life.

3. **Eat Mostly Protein and Vegetables:** If you have a set measure of your calorie intake, technically you can eat anything if you stay in that limit. However, not all calories are the same. We need protein to build muscle after exercise, and vegetables have fibre and all sorts of good nutrients. These two food groups also create the most satiety, which means if you eat these, you won't feel hungry again very soon. A 500-calorie snack could be one big packet of chips. To make up

500 calories, you can also have a 200-gram piece of grilled chicken and 500 grams of broccoli and other green vegetables. The packet of chips, while yummy, will make you feel hungry in one hour. The chicken and broccoli meal will keep you going for many more hours. These are extreme opposite examples, but you get the idea.

Also, when you eat vegetables, the fewer accompaniments you add to those vegetables—for example, oil, starch, chutneys and gravies—the better. This is particularly true of Indian food, where so many things are added to vegetables that their nutritional essence is lost. Palak patta (spinach leaves) are super healthy, but palak patta chaat, often found in many Indian restaurants, for which the palak leaves are dipped in batter made of gram flour, and deep fried, and drizzled with chutney, is not healthy. Gajar (carrots) are a fantastic health food, but only in their raw or steamed form. Gajar halwa, I don't need to tell you, is quite unhealthy. I'm sure I will be attacked for such opinions. Someone's mother must be making a super healthy gajar ka halwa. I'm not going to argue with that. If you are serious about your fitness, be honest with your diet, eat healthy for the most part and you are good.

4. **Limited Unhealthy Treats:** Life is always going to be full of tasty, tempting food options. There will be parties, dinners, festivals, birthdays, anniversaries

and, of course, the fridge and snack cupboard in your own house. Mithai, pizzas, samosas, chips, jalebis, candies, instant noodles, sugary drinks and bakery items will somehow end up near you. You will be tempted. These foods are delicious and fun. The problem is all these items are major calorie bombs. These dense, sugary food items are digested fast and make you feel hungry quickly. One laddoo can have as many calories as two big rotis and a bowl of daal. While a laddoo is tastier than daal and roti, it will not only mess up your calorie count for the day but also make you feel hungry again very soon.

What is one to do then when tempted? There is no clear answer. If you are an extremely motivated and disciplined person, you will make these treats extremely rare. I heard John Abraham's favourite sweet is kaju katli. He once mentioned in an interview that he hasn't touched kaju katli for eleven years! I also heard that another top actor only smells sweets and doesn't eat them! I am not that guy. And chances are neither are you. If you were, you would be superfit and not need to read this chapter. You may not be able to give up sweets for eleven years, but can you give them up for eleven days? Can you make dessert a once-a-week affair? Or twice a week at best? That too, ensure you eat a reasonable, small portion? That's what you need to do if you want to stick to a healthy diet. Are unhealthy food items the exception or the norm in your life? The only person who can honestly answer this question is you. One good rule I read about was the 'one-treat-every-forty-eight-hours' rule, where you eat something unhealthy once in two days, or every forty-eight hours. That way, you are never more than twenty-four hours away from having had a treat or from having a treat. Sounds doable, doesn't it?

3. Exercise

The third and most visible pillar of fitness is exercise. Sleep and a healthy diet have few visuals. Exercise has hundreds. Instagram is full of guys and girls flexing in the gym, running outdoors, climbing mountains, swimming, or doing different kinds of physical activities. Exercise is important. Human bodies are meant to move on a regular basis. Today, hundreds of fitness instructors and experts run YouTube channels, apps and websites where you can get different exercise plans. Thousands of articles on the internet cover this topic as well. However, if, like me, all of this only confuses you more, here are the broad parameters of an exercise plan you can follow. Note that this (along with everything else in the book) is not just meant for you to read. You have to *act* on it, and *implement* it in your life.

A Simple Exercise Plan

Simply put, exercise can be divided into cardio and weight training. People have different aesthetic, endurance and strength goals. Hence, their exercise routine may be planned accordingly. However, here is an exercise routine that works for most normal people:

1. **Exercise Daily (almost):** There is a lot of debate on how many days a week we need to work out. The answer is simple—most days. 'Most days could mean six days a week with one day of rest. Or, it could be all seven days a week, with the seventh day being a relatively lighter exercise day. Remember, any movement helps. Even a long walk counts. Your exercise session should be typically between forty-five minutes to an hour. This is a reasonable length of time to work out, and something you can stick to on most days. Some experts say three days a week of exercise is enough. I would recommend making movement a regular part of your life. As a bonus, the calories you burn during exercise get added back to your calorie quota, so you get to eat a bit more!

2. **Total Time of Exercise Per Week:** If your daily workout spans forty-five to sixty minutes, six days a week, it translates to 270 to 360 minutes per week of exercise. This is a good target to aim for and will

have significant physical and mental health benefits if consistently followed over time.

3. **Split Total Time between Cardio and Weight Training:** Roughly a half and half split of cardio and weight training works well, though you may tweak this based on your individual goals, requirements and preferences. Cardio involves activities that increase your heart rate, such as running, working out on the elliptical trainer, cycling, swimming, walking, climbing stairs and rowing machines. Get your heart rate to a level where you can feel some exertion, but not to dangerous levels. For weight-training days, train various large muscle groups of your body—upper body (chest, biceps, triceps, lats, delts), core (abdomen and back) and lower body (legs, glutes). There are tons of videos on exercises for the same, though often the best way is to stick to the basics and do compound lifts, which are discussed in the next point.

4. **Doing Basic Compound Lift Exercises:** Fancy exercise moves evolve all the time, but the basics work well and have stood the test of time. The classic weight training exercises are pull-ups, deadlifts, squats and bench presses. The charts below show these exercises, but I encourage you to look them up in videos on the internet or ask your gym trainer to show them to you. These basic exercises look simple. However, they involve a fair amount of form,

technique and precautions that must be followed to prevent injuries. Also, go slow on adding more load. Don't compete with bodybuilders. Push yourself a bit every day, while listening to your body.

Squats   Deadlifts   Pullups

Bench Press   Overhead Press   Dips

Barbell Row   Seated Arnold Press

THE COMPOUND LIFTS

5. **Run:** If you can, run. Personally, I love running. Your cardio workout can be a run, at least on some days. A good run is like taking a bath on the inside. Your blood circulation improves, and so do your mood,

confidence and energy levels. Running doesn't need a lot of equipment or a gym. Start slow, with moderate distances. I started running properly at forty-seven. I can now run fast for reasonably long distances. My typical run now is 8 kilometres, three times a week (the remaining days are for weight training or swimming). Occasionally, I take part in 10 kilometre runs, which involve road races in a city. From being a fat guy a few years ago, I completed my last 10 kilometre run in forty-seven minutes and twenty seconds, which people tell me is a pretty good speed. Again, if *I* can, *you* can! Run whatever distance you are initially comfortable with. Gradually increase speed and distance until you can run at a good pace for forty-five minutes to an hour.

6. **If You're Not Going to a Gym, Do Body-Weight Exercises:** Push-ups, sit-ups, jumps, running, squats, lunges—these are just a few of the exercises that don't require any equipment. Look up videos on body-weight exercises or no-gym workout. If you cannot afford a gym or don't have one near you, it's no excuse. Work out anyway.

7. **Mix It Up and Stretch:** A final tip is to mix up your exercises, both to cut boredom and keep giving the body new challenges. Working out often contracts your muscles. Hence, after every workout, stretch for a few minutes. Better still, make one of the workout days a yoga day. Yoga is amazing for stretching your

> body, and the right asanas, done at a good pace (brisk Suryanamaskars, for instance), can even become your workout for that day.

This first rule has a lot packed into it. Fitness demands your attention every single day of your life. However, it also pays off spectacularly. If you want to be a top 1 per cent person in this world, you must incorporate fitness in your life. It will train you to be tough and help fight all the battles life may bring your way.

....

Key Takeaways

- To achieve anything in life, fitness should be your number one priority.

- Fitness comprises three aspects—a healthy diet, physical exercise and good quality sleep.

- You have to silence that 'loser' voice, which urges you to relax and not work hard.

- Exercise builds your ability to do hard things, even outside the gym.

- Maintaining a healthy diet helps build discipline and patience, and resist temptation—qualities that help in life as well.

- A simple but effective fitness plan is all you need to look and feel good.

....

'I'm so fat,' Viraj said.

'Excuse me?' I said.

'I am fat. Not fit,' Viraj said. 'See.' He clutched the sides of his stomach.

'Physically, you mean. What about mentally?'

After a pause, Viraj said, 'I'm not mentally fit either. Unable to sleep. Stalking Arpita. Calling her thirty times. Making a fool of myself.'

'What is stopping you from taking care of your fitness?'

'Work keeps me so busy. I have no time to exercise. No money to maintain a healthy diet either.'

I did not respond. He would know from my expression I wasn't convinced.

'It's true. Stop looking at me like that,' he said. 'I don't have a life like yours where I can count calories or spare an hour to exercise.'

'Unlock your phone,' I said.

'What?'

'Go to your screentime. Do it. Now.'

Viraj opened the screentime app on his phone. His screentime was a massive ten hours per day. Understandably, the most used app was Zomato, at five hours daily.

'That's work,' Viraj said. 'Whenever I get an order or am out for delivery, I have to use it.'

'Sure. What about the remaining five hours? Three hours a day on Instagram!'

'Wow, three hours? That must be a mistake,' Viraj said with a sheepish expression.

'It isn't. You spend three hours on Instagram daily. Doing what?'

'Nothing much. Just scrolling, chilling whenever I have free time.'

'But you don't have forty-five minutes to run every day, right?'

Viraj looked up from his screen to make eye contact with me. I continued. 'That's how you chill? By scrolling through reels? Instead of doing push-ups, or even just sleeping early to get a proper night's rest?'

Viraj did not answer. I spoke again.

'Let's talk about your healthy diet. How expensive are carrots? Or cucumbers? Or eggs? They probably cost the same, or only a little more than vada pav and samosas, right?'

'Healthy food takes time to prepare ...' Viraj started but paused mid-sentence.

'Let's see what else you browse apart from Instagram. There's YouTube, Facebook and, what's that, Pornhub? Another hour there. But no time to cut carrots for ten minutes? Or boil some eggs?'

Viraj turned his head sideways to look away from me.

'Say something,' I said in a firm voice.

'Fine. I am making excuses. I could do it if I cared enough.'

'You must. Fitness is the first of the eleven rules. You have to follow them all. You want to cross your aukaat, right? Or do you want to beg Arpita to take your call?'

'I do. I want to cross my aukaat.'

'Good. Run. Lift heavy things. Eat more natural foods. Don't eat crap. Respect yourself and your body.'

Viraj remained silent.

'I made the same mistake, Viraj,' I said. 'I never exercised when I was young. I blamed everything else, made amazing excuses. Led me nowhere.'

'You said you had a rough childhood?' Viraj said.

'I did. My father believed in violence. I was frequently beaten up. He also fought with my mother. Never gave her money to run the house. We almost never had money. There were constant shouting fests in the house.'

'And the neighbour ... that boy?'

I looked up at Viraj.

'What?' Viraj said.

'I have never spoken about that to anyone.'

'You don't have to,' Viraj said.

We remained silent for a minute. I took a deep breath and began to speak.

'I was ten. Didn't know properly what was happening to me. He was fifteen. Said he would teach me a few things. I didn't realize they were inappropriate. It went on for a few years. Now, is your curiosity satisfied or do you need more details? About what a fifteen-year-old boy can make a ten-year-old do?'

'I'm sorry. I didn't mean to—'

'It's okay. You wanted to know, that's fine. And I am sorry I snapped at you. It's really hard for me to talk about this.'

'I understand. You didn't have to.'

'You have been revealing some very personal details about yourself. It only seems fair I do the same.'

'But this ...' Viraj said and paused mid-sentence.

'What?'

'I just ... I'm surprised.'

'By what?'

'I thought you have this nice house. And that you have always had it. And you became a writer from here.'

'No. I didn't. I didn't have easy circumstances at all. But I try not to complain about them. I don't make excuses. There's no point, is there? Excuses don't help in changing things and making them better.'

'No. I will start running from today itself. And won't eat junk food.'

'Great. I think we are done for the day.'

Talking to him felt a little overwhelming for me today. Normally, I was the stronger of the two of us. Today, it was the other way around.

'You okay, sir ... Chetan?' he said in a concerned voice.

'Yes. Tough to go back to the past. But glad I did. Especially if it helped you realize where I have come from to get here. We all have a backstory.'

'Thank you for sharing it with me. And trusting me.'

'Aren't you trusting me as well? I am only doing the same.'

He came forward and gave me a hug.

'You are very strong, sir.'

'Not always. I try,' I said.

'Yes. What is the next rule?'

'*You have to wait until tomorrow. What will you bring me for lunch?*'

'*Whatever you wish, sir. I can recommend a good south Indian place.*'

────※────

My doorbell rang at 1 p.m. Viraj handed me the food packets as soon as I opened the door.

My lunch had come from Madras Diaries. I had ordered a pesarattu green moong dal dosa and steamed idlis. The smell of ghee wafted through the air as I opened the packet. I opened the little cups of chutney—coconut, tomato and tamarind.

'*This looks great, thanks for the recommendation,*' I said, '*but it is too much. You have to help me finish all this.*'

'*Okay. But I will have just one idli.*'

'*Just one?*'

'*Counting calories.*'

'*Great, Viraj. Sit down. Ready for the second rule?*' I said.

'*Absolutely!*' Viraj seemed all set.

I poured the sambar into two small steel bowls. I passed a bowl of sambar and an idli to him.

I tore off a piece of the green moong daal dosa and dipped it in sambar.

'*This is so good,*' I said, taking a bite.

'*I told you.*'

'*It's great, thank you! Anyway, now for Rule Two.*'

RULE #2

MASTER YOUR EMOTIONS

*'The wise man is master of his emotions, and
the fool is their slave.'*

—EPICTETUS

**Screw your own feelings. But learn to read other
people's feelings well.**

One of the fundamental aspects of being human is
our emotional nature. We think with what can be
broadly understood as the logical, rational part of the
brain. However, we feel things through the emotional part
of the brain. Scientists have identified specific areas of the
brain that perform these functions. When I tell you to
add ten and fifteen, a part of your brain quickly performs
the calculation and tells you the answer: twenty-five. If I
ask you what the capital of India is, your brain taps into
a memory centre and pulls out the answer: New Delhi.

These are rational, logical activities. The brain
performs these important functions and helps us do well

in life. If a woman is in the business of making shirts, for instance, she will need her logical brain to estimate the cost of making a shirt. This includes the individual cost of fabric, buttons, thread and the stitching charges of the tailor. The rational part of the brain will also determine the price at which the shirt can be sold to make a decent profit. A sharp, rational brain helps you excel at what you do.

However, having a fantastic logical brain is not enough to live a wholesome life. You must consider the role of the part of the brain that governs the emotions. While its functions are key to basic survival, it is also the reason why most people win or fail. If you can control your emotional brain, then coupled with a good logical brain, it will multiply your accomplishments. On the contrary, if you let your emotions control you, they can destroy your life.

Most human beings cannot control their emotions, or at least find it hard to do so. To see why this is the case, it is important to understand what emotions are.

Our emotions emanate from the primitive part of our brain, often known as the hindbrain or the lizard brain. The limbic cortex is the part of the brain that we call the lizard brain, because, as Dr Joseph Troncale, an Addiction Medicine physician at START—Certified Community Behavioral Health Clinic, York, Pennsylvania, puts it, 'the limbic system is about all a lizard has for brain function.'[2] Troncale summarizes the functions of the limbic system as the fight-or-flight response, the need for food and sex, and the freeze response we sometimes get when we're too scared to fight or flee. This is our emotional brain. Our rational brain (and only human brains have evolved to this degree), was an add-on to this primitive brain, and exists in the frontal part of our brain. The primitive brain is wired to make us act faster than the rational one. When we face certain stimuli or situations, the primitive brain sends crude-but-fast signals and sensations to certain parts of our body. This bodily sensation or physiological response to a thought or observation makes it an emotion. When you add ten and fifteen and get twenty-five, you don't 'feel' anything in your body. However, if you have not eaten for a while and I place a plate of hot gulab jamuns in front of you, you will 'feel' it in parts of your body. You will salivate, your gut will contract a bit and you will want to eat the food. At this point, your rational brain, which knows how much sugar the gulab jamuns have, will be sidestepped and you will gobble up dessert. However, if you have control over your emotions, you will gently move the plate aside.

We have similar emotional responses to all sorts of things in life—a food item, a person (particularly a romantic partner), a fun activity (like a party invitation), a tough task ahead (like the lack of motivation to go to the gym) or when we feel rejection (at a job or in love).

Emotions are also involved when we exhibit racism, or communalism, or casteism. Our primitive brain seeks safety in 'people like us' versus 'people like them'. This emotion is fully exploited by political parties when they seek votes in the name of identity. Logically, we know we should elect politicians based on their ability to govern and develop the nation. However, come election time, emotions rule. Hordes of people vote based on identity. We allow ourselves to get fat, date the wrong people, waste time on useless relationships, waste our careers, elect unworthy leaders and do a lot of stupid things in the name of emotions.

Some of our behaviours are stupid indeed from a rational point of view. However, the emotional brain doesn't find them stupid. It merely acts on instinct and the bodily sensations it perceives *at that time*. Hence, it can make you take decisions and actions that do not serve you in the future. So, what 'felt right' emotionally at a particular instance ends up feeling quite stupid in the long term. The majority of humans allow themselves to be ruled by their emotions. That is why most of humanity is not successful in life. The small percentage of people who control their emotions and understand the emotions of other people end up ruling the world. It is really that simple. If you want to do well in life, you must learn to rein in your emotions.

Here's a two-step process to mastering your emotions.

Step 1: Identify Your Current State of Mind

While all of us have a brain comprising two parts, one that thinks rationally and one that processes information emotionally, people vary in terms of which part of the brain dominates their life. How do we make decisions or choose our actions? Are our decisions and choices primarily based on reason or on emotion? The chart below shows the various illustrative archetypes of people in terms of rational vs emotional dominance.

100% Rational   Rationally Dominant   Emotionally Dominant   100% Emotional

Rational Emotional

TYPES OF BRAIN

What Type of Brain Do You Currently Have?

1. ***100 Per Cent Rational:*** The diagram on the extreme left represents a 100 per cent logical and rational brain. This is an extreme example of a person who has no emotions and decides everything on a rational, calculated and logical basis. Some people mistakenly believe that this is what it means to have emotional control—be 100 per cent rational. I'm sure

you have heard people who have been emotionally hurt say, 'Oh, from now on I don't want to have any emotions.' However, emotional control doesn't mean killing all emotions—that would be akin to killing an essential part of being human. What's the point of life if you don't feel anything? What if you never felt joy, happiness, love or pleasure? Such a life isn't even worth living. The point is to control emotions so they serve you, rather than letting them mislead you into living a disastrous life. You don't want to be this person. It's okay to feel those emotions. Just don't be ruled by them.

2. **Rationally Dominant:** The second type is the rationally dominant but still somewhat emotional brain. This is where you want to be. Here, both the rational and the emotional parts exist. However, it is the rational part that dominates. The emotional brain screams in the morning, not wanting to get out of the warm quilt and go to the gym. Yet, the rational brain kicks in and tells the emotional brain in a calm voice, 'Dude, we are doing this. This is what we do now. We wake up on time and exercise.' Hearing this, the emotional brain doesn't protest anymore. It shuts up and you get on with your day. That's how people with rationally dominant brains operate.

Say the emotional brain wants to quit preparing for a tough entrance exam over two years. It screams, 'It's too hard! Let's quit!' or, 'I don't have it in me!' or, 'It's okay to not do so well in life, let's just scroll through Instagram instead of studying.' However, the dominant rational brain counters this. 'Watching a web series and not studying won't serve my future. Sorry, emotional brain, I'm going to give up immediate pleasure and do the hard work. Don't disturb me. I won't let you win anyway.' The emotional brain then relents, becomes quiet. Eventually, the emotional brain even supports your goal. It might provide joyful emotions of accomplishment after you finish studying a chapter. If your brain is not like this at present, it needs work. Don't worry, it can be fixed. However, this won't happen automatically or in a day. You will have to fight and train the emotional brain every day, until it finally realizes what it is dealing with. It's dealing with a beast called you, with a rational brain that is smart and tough. You can't give up. Your focus has to be set on your long-term goals and you have to completely block the desire for immediate or short-term pleasure.

3. ***Emotionally Dominant***: This is the kind of brain that most humans have. Let's say these people are EmDoms. They do possess a logical brain, but their emotional brain totally dominates it. If you live your life based on 'how you feel' about things, this is you, my friend. You study if you *feel like it*, you exercise only if you 'feel like it', and if you *feel like*

it', you apply for a better job, and if you *'feel like it'* doing it that day you do it that day. Well, Mr/Ms Only-If-I-Feel-Like-It, you are the total opposite of the rationally dominant person, who will do it whether he or she feels like it or not. Because, on most days, you won't *'feel like'* doing the hard things. EmDoms can also get swayed by others easily. The moment their emotional buttons are pressed, they get *'triggered'* and are led in that direction. That's why millions get swayed by politicians making emotional speeches that have no relevance to the development of their village, city, state or country.

> You will have to fight and train the emotional brain every day, until it finally realizes what it is dealing with. It's dealing with a beast called you, with a rational brain that is smart and tough. You can't give up. Your focus has to be set on your long-term goals and you have to completely block the desire for immediate or short-term pleasure.

People become emotional about their siblings and give up property rights (which happens often in India, when women are sometimes expected to give up property rights for their brothers). Emotions make people have fights in public places, say things they should not say in office meetings, eat food they should not eat and take other actions that prove to be harmful for them. Most of humanity can be classified as EmDoms. This is the default state of the human condition. This is why most of humanity is Class III. Your goal in life is to shake out that EmDom part of you and not let emotions sway you. Instead, let your rational brain lead you to become the best possible person you can be.

4. ***100 Per Cent Emotional People:*** This is a category at the extreme end of the rational-emotional spectrum. This is a rare category (at least I hope it is!). These are the people who are completely swayed by emotions. They don't use any logic at all. These people are the most gullible and can be manipulated easily. They are used by those with rationally dominant brains as exploitable idiots. The people who get beaten up or end up in jail over some twisted ideology, such as supporters of terrorist organizations, would probably fall in this category. They are ready to ruin their lives over their leader's beliefs because those beliefs resonate with them emotionally. They don't realize that they have a lot to lose (sometimes even their lives), and that all the gains from their pains will go to the leader. They can't think like this because they have suspended all rationality and are solely driven by emotions. Often, one hears about people who have killed someone out of jealousy, or have ended their own lives for their lover or because of adverse circumstances—these are instances where, at least in that moment, these individuals have lost all

rationality. This lack of emotional control could even result from a mental ailment, and such people would need help to overcome their state of mind. However, the very point of describing this category is to show how bad things can get if you let your emotions rule you completely. So, do you know what type of brain you have right now?

Step 2: Resolve to Become a Rationally Dominant Person

If you have identified yourself as already being rationally dominant, great! If you have figured out that you are not, then thanks for being completely honest with yourself! Remember, it's okay to not be rationally dominant. Most people are not. Even I have let emotions get the better of me many times in my life. I have stayed up all night making mix tapes (back when we had audio cassettes, it did take all night to make a mix tape) for girls in my class in the eighth standard. Come to think of it, it was pretty stupid. The girl wasn't even my girlfriend; she was just a crush who took the mix tape and went on to date someone else! She probably would have spent time with him listening to all the romantic songs I had recorded for her!

Emotions are powerful. They swirl through us day and night. They make us who we are. I do love emotions. I just try my best to not let them run my life. My aim is not to make you emotionally vacant or cold. I just want you to not be ruled by emotions. If you have not listened to your rational brain, or have let it be dominated by your emotions, that is your default brain wiring right now. However, the wonderful thing about our brains is that they are neuroplastic. Our wiring (another way of saying our default thought patterns, narratives or mindset) can be changed. Slowly, with better choices and behaviours, you can 'rewire' these circuits. The brain will resist. You will feel uncomfortable, maybe even fail a few times and let your emotions get the better of you. But you can do it. Start with taking one decision, one action where you let your rational brain win. For instance, decide to take a 2 kilometre walk today. Then do it. Your emotional self may tell you not to do it. Do it anyway. Do any of these challenging things—go for a run, a walk, a gym workout, cut out sugar, study for two hours continuously. Do something that's hard for you but still doable, for five straight days.

After you have achieved this, have a conversation with yourself. Tell yourself, 'See, I could do it. My rational brain can lead the way.' Do it again, for three weeks this time. Study an extra hour, walk for forty-five minutes and push yourself. Train your brain to listen to and respect the logical part. Do it over and over until the wiring shifts. Soon it will feel natural

> **The wonderful thing about our brains is that they are neuroplastic.**

to follow your rational brain. In other words, becoming rationally led will become a habit. Congratulations, you are now rationally dominant.

Reading Other People's Emotions

While you work on your own emotional control, learn to read other people's emotions well too. As most of the human population is emotionally driven, there's value in learning what makes other people tick emotionally. This doesn't mean you become an emotional manipulator, or that you exploit other people's feelings. This simply means being sensitive to the fact that almost everyone you interact with is driven emotionally, at least partially so. Even a rational nuclear scientist working on cutting-edge quantum physics has emotional touchpoints. She probably wants to be recognized in her field. Or she feels hurt when the department head shoots down her idea for the next research project. Or she feels bad about staying in the lab for long hours and not spending enough time with her three-year-old child. When you are emotionally sensitive to other people, you see them differently. The nuclear physicist is not just a scientist, but a person. As is everyone around you—your family, friends, colleagues, waiters, auto drivers, the guy at the ticket counter, the shopkeeper and the delivery guy who brought you lunch. And, ultimately, knowing their emotional drivers will get you much further with them.

This doesn't mean you form deep emotional bonds with everyone you meet in this world. No, that would drain you. Emotions require energy, and you only have so much to give. However, just layer your interaction with a slight emotional touch. 'How's your son?' or 'You look tired today. Are you okay?' or 'How does this make you feel?' are all queries in the emotional realm. Being kind, sporting a smile and just attempting to make the person in front of you feel a little better are all examples of emotional caring. You need to use this soft emotional brush for others, while you yourself toughen up mentally, develop emotional control and become more rational.

....

Key Takeaways

- The small percentage of people who can control their emotions end up ruling the world. It's okay to feel emotions; just remember not to let them rule your life. Rein in your emotions if you want to go far.

- Train your brain to listen to and respect the logical way of thinking. Do this repeatedly until this way of thinking becomes a habit.

- Be sensitive, kind and caring in your approach to others but be mentally tough with yourself.

- Do things that you *need* to do to achieve your goals, not what you 'feel like' doing because your emotions tell you to do them.

■ If you can master your emotional brain, along with having a trained logical brain, your accomplishments will multiply. But, if you let your emotions control you, they can destroy your life.

....

'You are right. I am 100 per cent emotional. In other words, a fool and an idiot,' Viraj said.

'You are not a fool,' I said.

I opened the mini-Gujarati thali he had brought for me that day. The disposable plastic thali had eight slots, each for a different Gujarati dish—thepla, kadhi, daal, srikhand, aloo, ondhiyo and a few more things I couldn't recognize. It is amazing how innovative food delivery has become in the last few years.

I had a lot of writing work to finish. How do Gujarati people get any work done, I wondered. If I ate this entire thali, I would sleep all afternoon.

I slid the food aside. Viraj continued to speak.

'Why did I move to Mumbai? Because of my emotions for Arpita. Why did I call her dozens of times? Or stalk her and her friends and her boyfriend's social media for hours every day? It's just my stupid emotions that made me do these things.'

I went to my kitchen to keep the thali in the fridge. I decided I would have it for dinner. I came back to the dining room.

'I've done emotionally stupid things too,' I said.

'But I'm completely stupid emotionally. What is all this going to achieve for me? Nothing. Still, I can't seem to help myself.'

'See, you do have a rational brain. The voice that is telling you this is futile,' I said.

'Yes, I can hear that voice now. But mostly it's muted or weak.'

'You must learn to make that rational voice stronger. By doing things that you need to do, instead of what your emotions make you do.'

'I better go for a two-hour walk after work today. And no Instagram. And definitely no checking on Arpita or her new guy on Instagram.'

'Relax. One hour.'

'What?'

'A one-hour walk is enough. Don't overdo it. But yes, no more stalking.'

'Okay. I also must start running every morning. Half an hour at least.' Viraj seemed determined.

'Good. See you tomorrow.'

RULE #3

PUT YOURSELF FIRST

'If you don't put yourself first, who will?'

—MEL ROBBINS

**Live for yourself, not for others or to show
to others.**

Brace yourself. This rule may shake you up a little. Most people don't live for themselves. In fact, most people don't even understand what it means to live for themselves. However, if you want to get somewhere in life, jump right over that class barrier, be successful or even just be happy, you must be willing to do what is difficult for most people—put yourself first.

But what does it mean to put yourself first? What does it mean to live for yourself? Does it mean you become utterly selfish? Ignore, trample and use everyone around you to somehow get to the top? Become a psychopath? Ignore other people and their needs? Be greedy?

Wrong. All of the above is complete nonsense.

Let me explain with the help of an example.

You are sitting at home with your family on a Friday evening. You are a working professional. You have had a long tiring week at work. You want to stay at home, maybe just have soup for dinner. You also want to sleep by ten. The rest of your family, however, has different plans. Your parents want to go out for dinner at a new Indian vegetarian restaurant. Your spouse wants to go out too, but prefers to eat Chinese food and not have Indian again. Your children want to go to the mall and play in the video game arcade and have pizza later.

'Why don't we go to the mall?' your spouse suggests. 'That way the children can play video games, while we can eat in the food court, where everyone can get their choice of food from the various stalls.'

It seems like a great, win-win idea, you say to yourself.

Everybody begins to get ready. You do as well. After all, you want to make your family happy.

There is soup in the mall's food court, too, you think. Except, it isn't what you wanted. You wanted to stay home, have soup and sleep early. That way you could wake up early, feeling refreshed and go for a long run or an intense workout. Now you will have to drive to the mall, spend time there and drive back. It will be midnight by the time you get home. It's no big deal though, is it? Everyone does this for their family. This is what family bonding is, after all. You do things together. Everyone gets what they want and has fun as a unit. However, now you will wake up late. You won't have time to work out.

There are relatives coming home for lunch tomorrow. You will have to help in the preparations for that too.

The above episode is the story of every household. Except, I wonder if you noticed something? Amidst all the loud noise of what everyone else wanted, your voice saying what you wanted got drowned out. You didn't even seem to mind it. It happened automatically. Others said what they wanted, and you, being the super nice guy or girl you are, adjusted to the situation so that everyone else was happy. You didn't put yourself first.

However, that's a problem. Because, if *you* want to chase *your* happiness, *your* success and *your* dreams, *your* life has to be about *you*. You cannot live your life trying to please others and think that somehow in that process you will achieve all your goals as well. It is amazing how many people in the world, particularly in India, live to simply adjust to others. I did the same too. It took me a long time to realize this mistake.

When a choice is given to you in life, whose interests come to your mind first? Yours? Everyone else's? Suppose I tell you there's a job for you that pays double of what you're getting now, but you will need to move cities. What's the first, immediate impulse that

> If *you* want to chase *your* happiness, *your* success and *your* dreams, *your* life has to be about *you*. You cannot live your life trying to please others and think that somehow in that process you will achieve all your goals as well.

comes to your head? Is it: 'Oh, it is a great opportunity, but what about my kids' school? What about my parents? My friends circle?' Or: 'Damn, this is amazing! I'm so ready to go!'

For you to rise in life or even to be happy, it must be the latter. You need to reach a point where whatever happens, you think of yourself first. Your friends order a pizza at the restaurant. They pass it around. Your turn comes first to pick a slice. Do you take the best, biggest slice? Or do you take a smaller one so your friends can enjoy the rest? Well, take the best, biggest slice (if it's within your diet and fitness regimen allowance, of course!).

Consider making yourself the number one person in your life. You are the king, you are the queen. You matter the most. Love yourself so much that, no matter what, you will not compromise on your happiness, your needs.

Am I asking you to be an asshole? Not really. Though on a few occasions you may come across as one. However, it is imperative that you start thinking in this manner.

'But what about my relationships?' a voice in you will protest. 'Aren't friends and family important?' or 'How can I be a selfish prick? Shouldn't I be a giving person?'

Relax, breathe. I'm not saying relationships are not important. They are, and extremely so. Putting yourself first doesn't mean you *only* care for yourself and are ignorant of others. That's selfish. Protecting yourself isn't selfish, it's self-care. In an aeroplane, they ask you to put your oxygen mask on first and then help others. It's the same in life. If you don't place your needs first, how can you ever be there for others? Sure, the pizza slice was a trivial example. You could let the best slice go. But what about your life goals? Will you put those second too? Because when you spoil your sleep and skip your workout to go to the mall when you didn't want to, you are doing exactly that. Do that several times a week and you will suffer from chronic bad sleep, poor focus, bad performance at work and will fail to achieve your fitness and career goals. A purpose-driven person puts himself or herself first. You first, then others. That doesn't mean saying 'only me'. Rather, it's saying 'me first, then others'.

There is a great quote I once heard: 'Be yourself, the world will adjust.' This is what happens when you put yourself first. People will work around your needs. Over time, they will say, 'Oh, I know it is your sleep time, so you won't come to the mall now. It's okay, you rest and we will go without you, or we can all go together on Sunday.'

You see? How you set the boundaries of what is okay with you and what is not will ultimately signal to others to respect you and your needs. They will still get what they want, just not at the cost of your needs.

How I Stopped Being a People-Pleaser

I have been a people-pleaser all my life. I wanted to make everyone around me like me. In primary school, I used to learn jokes. I did this to make people laugh and feel happy when they were around me. Sounds cute, doesn't it? It was all fine until I reached a point where I couldn't stand anyone being even a little upset or disappointed with me. If I was doing something and they made the slightest face, it would ruin my mood. I extended this response to everything. At parties I would feel responsible for ensuring that everyone was having a good time, even if I wasn't the host. My energies were focussed on pleasing my relatives, friends and family. I would agree easily to whatever they said. Maybe that is why I became a writer ... to get people to like me. And even as a writer I used to feel the need to win over, impress and get validation from every critic who didn't like my book.

In all this, whatever *I* wanted was lost and buried. It came to a point where I didn't even know what I wanted in life. This, I realized later, is the case with a lot of people. Maybe it is this way with you too. If you don't know what you want, how can you ever get it? It took me decades to realize that this people-pleasing behaviour and constant attempts at getting validation is never-ending. I had to stop.

People-pleasing isn't just living your life *for* people. It is also about living your entire life to *show* people. For some reason, you want certain people to praise you, be in awe of you, or say, 'Wow, that's cool!' to everything you do. This makes you do jobs you hate, put on a persona that isn't really you, go after things that you think those people would like, not necessarily you. Before you know it, you are living a life that is a complete lie. You are no longer true to who you really are. You are not going towards goals that genuinely resonate with you. Your life is a puppet show, and you are the puppet dancing at the end of invisible strings that are controlled by other people The funny thing is those other people may not even know that they are controlling you, and may not even have that intention. Yet, you spend years of your life trying to win their validation.

Me as a Puppet

When I became a writer, I quit my banking job. All my friends, however, remained in banking. Bankers are about money, and the question they would ask me most was: 'How much money do you make as a writer?' The answer back then, when I had just started out was: 'Not much.'

I didn't become a writer to just make money. If I wanted to make money, I would have remained a banker.

However, somewhere, my friends' questions bothered me. I wanted to 'show them' that I could 'make a lot of money' as a writer too. In the process, over the next decade, I nearly killed myself with work—innumerable motivational talks, hundreds of flights a year, books, films, columns, TV appearances and even reality shows (gosh, why, I now wonder!). I worked at breakneck speed to maximize my earnings. I became fat, lost my health and, most importantly, lost sense of the main purpose of my writing life which was to express myself. It took the Covid-19 pandemic to jolt me back to reality. All of a sudden, a lot of my work—talks, flights, launches and film shoots—came to a grinding halt. The forced pressing of the pause button due to the pandemic gave me a chance to reflect on my life and see who I truly am. I realized that the friends who asked me how much money I make don't matter. It's my life. I must live it according to what I want. My friends probably don't even know till date the inner turmoil their harmless question caused in me.

I have managed to heal myself from this lifelong people-pleasing trap. Now, I try to live for myself. For instance, I wanted to write a book solely to help others. That's the voice that came from my heart. I felt people have enough sources of entertainment these days, but they need some guidance on how to make the most of their life. To write with a pure intention like this, and not for money, fame, people's expectations or any external marker of success, has helped me reach new levels of creative satisfaction and happiness. I believe eventually it will lead to more external success too.

....

Key Takeaways

- If you want to go after *your* happiness, *your* success and *your* dreams, *your* life most definitely has to be about *you*.

- Putting yourself first doesn't mean you care only for yourself. That's selfish. Protecting yourself isn't selfish, it's self-care.

- Set boundaries so that others learn to understand and respect your needs.

- Stop trying to please everyone—this will only cause you stress and encourage/allow others to control you.

- You can only make others happy if you are happy yourself.

....

Viraj came to see me the same evening, unannounced. He held a small icebox in his hand.

'Viraj? I didn't order anything.'

'I brought you ice-cream. A new restaurant was doing promotions. They gave these for free to delivery partners.'

He placed the brick-sized icebox on the table. Inside, there were two cups of strawberry ice-cream.

'But they gave them to delivery partners. They are meant for you,' I said.

'I want you to have it. As a gift. For whatever you are doing for me.'

He looked at me and smiled. I leaned forward and gave him a hug.

'Thank you,' I said.

'Besides, I'm on a diet,' he said, grabbing the sides of his stomach, 'these have to go.'

'Great. So you want me to get fat while you get fit?'

'No, no—'

'It's okay,' I said. 'I will be careful and eat in small portions.'

'I deleted Arpita's number, sir ... Chetan. Blocked her on Instagram. In fact, I deleted the Instagram app.'

'That's huge progress. How are you holding up?'

'It's tough. From now on, like you told me, I want to live for myself.'

'Nice.'

'Since this is a new visit, may I get the next rule?'

'We had a deal. One secret rule a day.'

'Please. One rule per visit. I can't wait.'

'Okay, just this one time. Let's talk about Rule Four. Master simple English.'

RULE #4

MASTER SIMPLE ENGLISH

'The English language is the language of international business, diplomacy, and culture. It is also the language of the internet and social media. Learning English will give you access to a world of opportunities.'

—BRITISH COUNCIL

You must have a good command over simple spoken and written English.

(*Note:* If you already have a decent command over English, feel free to skip this chapter. It won't hurt to read it though.)

I'm Indian. I grew up in Delhi speaking Hindi. I still speak and think in Hindi most of the time. However, I became a writer in English. Would my success and prominence as an Indian writer be the same if I wrote in Hindi? Would I be the same Chetan Bhagat?

I can't really say. I believe my ability to speak, read and write in English have given me access to places I wouldn't have had otherwise. I've sat at tables where I would not have had a chance to if I wrote in any other language. Would I have been invited to national-level conferences and conclaves? Would my profile as a columnist be the same if I didn't write for *The Times of India*, a leading English daily? Would I have made it to *Time* magazine's list of the 100 Most Influential People in the World?

In India, we talk to each other, listen to music and watch movies or TV shows in our mother tongues. Yet, we automatically slot people who speak English well in a higher category than those who don't. There are multiple historical reasons for this, most notably our colonization by the British for over 200 years. The British created an elite class of Indians who were proficient in English communication, both spoken and written. This helped them run the country. These elite Indians were paid well. They lived lavishly and had access to more opportunities, other powerful elite and fine things. It also made them appear more cultured, as the British promoted their culture as superior. When the British left, this English-speaking class remained. Their English-speaking kids grew up and took over the elite opportunities in newly independent India. They maintained the English-speaking elite bubble. That bubble has been pricked in recent years with increasing numbers of Indians entering the English-speaking world.

There are many other reasons for the superior status of English, which would require a separate long essay, maybe even another book, to discuss. For the purpose of this book, it should suffice to say that the pro-English bias exists even today. If you don't speak English well in India, certain opportunities and avenues are shut for you. It's as simple as that.

> If you don't speak English well in India, certain opportunities and avenues are shut for you.

No multinational will hire you. Top banking jobs will not open up for you. Employment at any officer-level position will be hard to get. Interviewers in many companies will laugh you out of the room if you fumble with your English. The quote at the start of the chapter which comes from the British Council (who of course have the mandate to promote English) is actually 100 per cent true.

Sure, there are examples of Indians who have made it big despite not having a good command over English. Many leading entrepreneurs, national-level sportspersons and movie stars have made it without knowing the language. However, these exceptions don't change the norm. The most common Iron Gate applied in India to prevent you from jumping over the class barrier is this one language—English.

It is important to understand that English speakers in India aren't all the same in terms of proficiency. For ease of understanding, I will classify them under three broad categories: E-0, E-1 and E-2.

1. ***The E-0s***: The E-0s are people who don't know or speak English at all. For those in this category, career choices can get extremely limited. In Japan or China, you can become the chairman of a bank even if you don't speak English. But you can't even become a bank branch manager in India without knowing English. You can become a blue-collar worker—a security guard, driver, cook, delivery boy or factory labour. You could become an electrician, plumber, mobile repair person, welder, foreman or even a factory shopfloor supervisor. Unfortunately, these professions in India don't pay very well, nor are they respected like white-collar jobs. In the US, a plumber or electrician can make up to USD 100,000 a year (₹83 lakhs at current exchange rates). Despite the US being a country with a higher cost of living, this is considered a good income there. In India, plumbers and other repairmen make much less than those in white-collar professions. This anomaly needs to be corrected. The politics of it is a separate issue. For now, you must remember that E-0s have it the hardest.

2. ***The E-1s:*** These are people who have learnt English but don't have native-level comfort with the language. This is the group that most Indians who learn English belong to. Incidentally, many of the readers of my books fall in this category. They have

made me a successful writer, and I thank them for that! The E-1s learnt English in school but were not exposed to much English at home. An E-1's school may have been an English-medium school or a vernacular-medium one where English is a compulsory subject. However, at home, the E-1s have a vernacular environment. While growing up, I was in this category. The knowledge of English helps E-1s, especially compared to E-0s, to find out about opportunities, understand science subjects better from better-quality English textbooks and take tough entrance exams. E-1s get selected for job interviews in better companies. If they are lucky enough to be judged by a panel comprising E-1s, they may even get the job.

However, E-1s can also falter and fail. This is because some E-1s know English but lack the confidence to communicate in it fluently. If their accent is shaky or their sentence construction is somewhat incorrect, it could lead to rejection at a dream job interview. That might mean relegation to a lower class of society. It's just a language but look at the power it has!

The repercussions of not knowing English reasonably well are huge. Note that 'reasonably well' doesn't mean Oxford-quality, rarefied, perfectly accented English. That isn't what is required. But you must be at a level where you can communicate fluently in English. More on how to do that later in the chapter.

3. *The E-2s:* The E-2s are a small category of Indians who grew up with English all around them. These people not only went to a good English-medium school, but were also surrounded by the English-speaking world when they grew up. Their

> The repercussions of not knowing English reasonably well are huge. Note that "reasonably well" doesn't mean Oxford-quality, rarefied, perfectly accented English. That isn't what is required. But you must be at a level where you can communicate fluently in English.

parents knew English (as high-level E-1s or E-2s themselves). They watched English TV programmes and movies while growing up. They read English newspapers, magazines and books. The uncles and aunts of E-2s spoke English too. Many of the E-2s' family friends were E-2s as well. This is the exclusive club of 'sophisticated' people in India. Usually, there's nothing particularly 'sophisticated' about them apart from a good, firm grasp on their English. E-2s' good knowledge of English and their ability to blend into other E-2 circles give them unique opportunities. Certain fields like fashion, media, English-language publishing and art particularly love E-2s. E-2s command immediate attention in India.

> ❧ A man or woman who speaks English well and confidently is automatically seen as competent, confident, superior and someone to be taken seriously. ❧

A man or woman who speaks English well and confidently is automatically seen as competent, superior and someone to be taken seriously.

It is somewhat nonsensical that these attitudes still exist more than seventy-five years after India's independence, but they do. I know Indian billionaires who get intimidated and impressed by a salesperson speaking English super-confidently. It is a stupid inferiority-complex residue from our colonial past. Fortunately, such attitudes are slowly receding. Today, too high a proficiency in English may also make you seem weird and alienate you. If you use esoteric words or speak in a clipped accent, you may not fit in well in an Indian work setting.

Your Goal: Master Simple English

The good news is you don't have to know E-2 level English. However, you must aim to become a confident, high-level E-1. Get your spoken English to a point where it is no longer a roadblock in life. Your written English must also be at a level where you can quickly compose an email, memo, covering letter, presentation or document in correct, coherent and easy-to-understand English. My writing style is essentially simple, easy and lucid English. It is what has made me one of the most popular writers in India. That is all you need—the ability to communicate in simple, effective English.

How to Build Competence in English

There is no shortage of tools available to learn English these days. There are books, apps, videos and courses all over the internet to help you become a better English speaker. These help to a certain extent.

However, the issue often isn't the knowledge of English. The issue is that you haven't lived in an English-speaking world or absorbed the culture of English speakers. You haven't relished English movies, music, TV shows and books. There haven't been people in your life with whom you could have discussions in English. In such a scenario, no matter how many online courses you complete, it will still show that you don't come from the English-speaking world. You won't have the same tonality, mannerisms and confidence when you speak the language. It's like learning to swim by watching videos and doing online courses. The moment you enter the swimming pool, the water you are in will hit differently.

> The issue often isn't the knowledge of English. The issue is that you haven't lived in an English-speaking world or absorbed the culture of English speakers.

And when you move from the swimming pool to the open sea, it will be a different ballgame altogether. Similarly, you must become good at the open-sea-swimming equivalent of English. And the only way to do that is relentless practice.

The resources available on the internet are a good starting point. See what you can afford, what suits your learning style or resonates with you. Go for it. When the course or video ends, you should ensure that you continue to practice. Here are some suggestions:

1. ***Interact with the World in English***: Did you go to the kirana store to buy bread? Well, ask for that bread in English. Are you at a restaurant? Order your food in English. Want to speak to a customer service representative on a call? Do it in English. You will fumble, make mistakes and then slowly correct yourself. Over time, English will start come to you naturally.

2. ***Talk to Family and Friends in English***: This can get tricky. The people who know you most can often judge you and hurt you the most too. This holds true especially with friends, who may laugh at you for your attempts to become this 'English' boy or girl. Your accent, grammar and sentences will go wrong. People will snigger as you speak. If a foreigner speaks a few words in broken Hindi, we applaud and ignore

their mistakes. However, when an Indian tries to learn English, we make fun of him or her. The shame one feels on being ridiculed can be humiliating enough to make one quit. But where is this shame coming from? Your emotional brain, isn't it? And since Rule Two told you to keep your emotions in control, that is what you will do. You will suck up the feelings of humiliation and apply your rational brain, which says, 'You need to master this language.' At the risk of being called such things as 'total idiot', you will continue to speak English at home all the time until you master it. You will say, 'I feel like having a glass of water. It's rather hot today,' even if people look at you like you have come from Mars or laugh at you because you seem like a wannabe.

> If a foreigner speaks a few words in broken Hindi, we applaud and ignore their mistakes. However, when an Indian tries to learn English, we make fun of him or her.

3. ***Read, Read, Read:*** Have you ever heard people describe someone as 'a well-TV-watched person' or 'a well-Instagram-reels-watched person'? No. They always say, 'a well-read person'. Books make you grow. They sharpen your mind and boost your creativity. Reading English books will flood your mind with English words and sentences and make

you increasingly comfortable with using them. Reading English books will make you look, feel and sound smart when you communicate in the language. Anyone who makes excuses about not reading ('Oh, but I'm not the reading type') is basically a lazy person. They don't want to make the mental effort required to read. Don't be lazy about this. Read!

4. *Think in English*: The key difference between E-2s and E-1s, or the people extremely comfortable in English and those who are not, is that E-2s think in English. When I ask you a question and tell you to respond in English, what do you do? If I ask whether you are free tomorrow evening, how does your mind process it? Do you first translate my question into your vernacular language, answer the question in that language in your head, and then translate it into English as you answer? This is how most Indians speak English. I used to do this too.

There's nothing inherently wrong in doing this. However, the extra steps of translating the input and output in your head will take more effort. This effort shows on your face, in your speech and the micro-seconds of delay as you answer the question compared to an E-2. Again, since you are translating the vernacular sentence in your head into English before you respond, you may end up using sentence structures of the language as you speak it instead of using the correct English syntax. For instance, when asked my name, I might say in Hindi, 'Main Chetan Bhagat hoon,' which if I literally translated into English would become: 'Myself Chetan Bhagat,' and it would be a dead giveaway that I'm not from the E-2 class. The correct English response is: 'My name is Chetan Bhagat.' If you think in English, you will not have this problem. Try to think in English. What's the weather like today? In your head, did you say, 'Thodi garmi hai,' or did you think, 'It is a bit hot,' in English? Similarly, think of the colour of the walls, the vehicles passing on the road and the world around you—all in English. Gradually, you will find that your response to the everyday world around you will get smoother in English, just as it is in your mother tongue, and communication in the language whenever it is needed will become easier and less stressful too.

5. *Get Help*: There's a lot you can do by yourself to master English, but don't hesitate to get help too. Join the best in-person English classes you can find around you and afford. Look online for practice apps for spoken English. There are apps such as Cambly that connect you to native English speakers around the globe to give you feedback.

Make it a priority to learn English. Don't let this already harsh world become harsher because you

> ❝ Make it a priority to learn English. Don't let this already harsh world become harsher because you can't string together words in a particular language. ❞

can't string together words in a particular language. Know that the mere knowledge of English is not enough. You need to be proficient and well-read, think in English and be fluent when you speak the language. This will unshackle you and open a world of opportunities that were previously closed to you.

....

Key Takeaways

- Reading, writing and speaking English well is crucial to getting ahead in anything you do.

- Get your English communication skills to a point where the language is no longer a roadblock in life.

- Your written English must be good enough to quickly compose an email, memo, cover letter, presentation or document in correct and easy-to-understand English.

- Though there are many resources freely available on the internet, it is most important to relentlessly practise speaking, reading and thinking in English.

....

'I know English. But I'm not good at it,' Viraj said.

'So get better,' I said.

He had brought me my order of avocado toast, which he said was a Bandra favourite, especially among people in the film industry. I couldn't understand how spreading a mashed bland fruit on a slice of toast made it worth 600 rupees, but the hype around avo-toasts meant I had to give it a try. The toast was smaller than a pack of cards. I could tell it wouldn't be enough for my lunch.

'The problem is, nobody in my town or home spoke in English. If only they spoke English around me, I would have known better English.'

'The trouble is, Viraj, you still blame other people or circumstances for your problems,' I said.

He looked up at me, surprised.

I continued. 'Many people live life saying this. It's a template sentence: if only others behaved better, my life would be better.'

'What?'

'That's the template. Of the victimhood argument.'

'Victimhood?'

'Yes. That you see yourself as a victim. Someone or something else is always responsible for your bad situation. You may even be right. Nobody spoke English in your town. So what? You can't get better until you do something about it. You can only control yourself. Not others or other situations.'

'Yes, that is true.'

'*If English is* your *weak spot,* you *have to do something about it.*'

'*You don't understand,*' *Viraj said.*

'*See, now it's about me. You think I don't understand how tough it was for you. Okay, I don't. It's my fault. Now what? How does that help you or tell you what to do next?*'

'*Okay, I get it. It's not your fault, but mine. I didn't pay attention to learning English. I will fix it,*' *Viraj said.*

'*Great. That's the way it should be. See you tomorrow with the next rule,*' *I said as I lifted the tiny box.* '*And with more food.*'

'*Yes. What's tomorrow's rule about?*'

'*Dopamine.*'

'*Dopa-what?*'

'*Let's talk tomorrow.*'

RULE #5

NO CHEAP DOPAMINE

*'The pleasure of the moment is the poison
of the future.'*

—CHINESE PROVERB

**Dopamine is a crucial neurochemical that regulates
your brain's motivation-and-reward circuit. Do not
mess with it. Dopamine-based rewards must only
come after effort. Any other reward is stolen.
Earn that dopamine, don't steal it.**

Understanding Dopamine

Many people have heard about the neurochemical dopamine produced in our brain. However, few understand what it really is. Two excellent books that talk about dopamine in detail are *Dopamine Nation*[3] by Anna Lembke and *The Molecule of More*[4] by Daniel Z. Lieberman and Michael E. Long. However, let me try to explain, in a concise manner, what dopamine is.

Your brain is a complex piece of biological machinery, with several separate parts operating many crucial circuits. Parts of the brain, for instance, regulate your motor movement. When you want to move your hand, your brain signals your intention by passing electrical currents through nerves to the hand muscles, which then initiate the movement. Among the brain's many amazing components is the dopaminergic system, which involves the production and secretion of dopamine. While dopamine plays a role in the proper functioning of our motor movements and memory, it also regulates our motivation, or our desire, to do almost anything. When you eat delicious food, it feels good. You want more of it, which makes you walk up to the buffet table to get more food. When you have sex, or even if someone you're attracted to kisses or cuddles you or says loving words to you, it feels pleasurable. You want more of it. Hence, people make concerted efforts to find a lover or be in a relationship. When you have alcohol, it gives you the feeling of relaxation. You want more of it.

Notice the common thread of 'want more of it' in the above examples. This 'wanting more' is dopamine at work. Whenever you like something and the body demands more of it, it is a result of the release of dopamine while you are performing that activity. In that sense, dopamine isn't just the neurochemical responsible for experiencing pleasure, but rather it is the neurochemical that results in us *wanting more*. The dopamine in your brain motivates you to seek more of whatever gives you pleasure. Why is knowing all this important? Because today we live in a world where a lot of cheap dopamine is available. We live in times where triggering a dopamine release can be as easy as drinking a bottle of beer. Or smoking. Or eating sugary foods. Or watching adult content. Or scrolling on Instagram (yes, even that releases dopamine).

What's wrong with it, you might ask. What is so bad if we enjoy something, and the brain asks for more of it?

The problem is that all these cheap dopamine releases require very little effort. There's not much work in opening an adult site and masturbating for an orgasm. There's no hard pursuit involved in smoking a cigarette, and then lighting up another one. Pouring a glass of wine and sipping it doesn't require you to toil for the entire day. Eating sugary food is easy too. All of these trigger dopamine releases without you exerting any effort. If you waste away your precious dopamine on these easy activities, how will you ever get the dopamine that makes you want to truly work hard? Cheap dopamine release methods are now available everywhere. They mess up your brain's effort and reward system. Why slave in the gym for an hour every day when you can feel good by drinking beer and munching on French fries? Why study an extra chapter of physics at night, when you can play video games instead? Why work on your new business, when you could just smoke cigarettes and scroll through Instagram all evening?

It is important to understand that it was never meant to be this way. Our brain circuits have evolved over millennia. There was a time when humans had to venture into the wilderness, walk barefoot on stony ground or among thorny bushes for hours and risk being attacked by wild animals in the hope of finding a fruit or a small animal to eat. If they didn't, there would be no lunch or dinner. There was a lot of physical effort required to get access to food. The pleasure of eating came after a long, hard pursuit. Today, all we have to do is open the kitchen cupboard or fridge and get our hands on whatever we want to eat.

This is how your brain gets messed up when you allow loads of cheap dopamine in your life. How can I, or anyone else, motivate you to put in genuine effort when feeling pleasure and satisfaction is so easy? Opening a bottle of alcohol or stuffing your face with food doesn't lead to any tangible accomplishment. Real achievements in life only come from real striving.

Dopamine Tolerance

As if messing up your brain reward circuits was not enough, here's another problem with cheap dopamine fixes. The pleasure you get from cheap dopamine reduces over time. Ask a regular smoker. The first few cigarettes they ever had gave them a high or a kick, which just doesn't happen anymore. Most smokers eventually only smoke to avoid the withdrawal symptoms that come with nicotine addiction. If they don't smoke, they get headaches or feel other forms of discomfort and can't focus. There is no longer any sort of pleasure associated with it. It is the same when it comes to watching porn. One gets desensitized over time and needs more and more stimulation to compensate for decreasing levels of pleasure. Food and social media scrolling work the same way as well. After a point it's not about feeling pleasure, it's about managing an addiction. You do it to avoid the negative symptoms—craving, boredom, etc. Hence, you are in a trap. This kind of cheap dopamine release not only destroys your motivation and reward circuit, but it also makes you an addict and takes away any real pleasure from any activity. It ruins your brain and your life.

> **The pleasure you get from cheap dopamine reduces over time.**

Today, cheap dopamine is being pushed at you by large multinational companies who are raking in profits in the process. Somebody is making money even as you become addicted to their products—cigarettes, junk food, alcohol, pornography, video games, social media sites—which are all doing the same thing to your brain.

They are providing cheap, harmful dopamine. Stop! Don't get trapped and waste your life to serve these corporate interests.

With big global corporations spending billions of dollars only to lure you into their dopamine trap, it is indeed challenging to quit it. Your brain will always seek the easy path to enjoyment or pleasure. It is always in search of instant, short-term gratification. What can I do right now to 'feel' good? Before you know it, the answer will lead you to a cookie or a drink or Instagram reels or, essentially, a cheap dopamine fix.

How to Quit the Pursuit of Cheap Dopamine

The first step is to understand why you are quitting cheap dopamine in the first place. It is because you need to restore your natural effort and reward connection. I'm not asking you to become like the Stone Age man and forage for food. No, please use all modern conveniences like the fridge and sliced bread. However, make sure a big part of your waking day is composed of working hard at doing something productive.

> The brain is always in search of instant, short-term gratification. What can I do right now to "feel" good? Before you know it, the answer will lead you to a cookie or a drink or Instagram reels or, essentially, a cheap dopamine fix.

This could be your studies, exercise routine, cleaning your room, making important work calls, researching for your next job, working on your business idea or whatever else is a part of your grind. Most of your day's activities should involve some effort and be aligned to your long-term goals. Cheap dopamine activities, which may be fun, should be done in moderation.

Managing My Own Cheap Dopamine

Cheap dopamine temptations surround and affect me as well. My current goals are to get fitter and to write this book. Ideally, a big part of my day should be composed of working towards achieving these goals. Apart from this, I also have other routine but important work like filing my taxes, managing my investments, running various errands and completing office administrative tasks, replying to emails and perhaps packing for the next trip. I have to put effort into all this as well. None of these activities give me the instant reward of a high, though I do feel some satisfaction if I have a productive day of work. The cheap highs are everywhere though. I feel like scrolling through Insta reels or finding out what's happening on X (formerly Twitter) or checking WhatsApp fifty times a day. I don't need to. It doesn't serve me. Yet, I keep getting drawn to these activities due to those tiny hits of cheap dopamine. In turn, my work slows down. In fitness too, I crave a cookie with my coffee or feel like having a drink with friends in the evening. All this will go against my fitness goals. And yet, the cheap dopamine these activities release makes me keep wanting to do them.

I have tried to manage all this by using the magic word—moderation. I work. I also make it a point to relax and take a break. I do watch what I eat. But now and then I indulge too. If I meet friends, I either skip alcohol or drink in moderation. I scroll through social media, but I'm aware this is not good for me and again apply the magic word—moderation. My goals remind me to manage my cheap dopamine, and it is a daily pursuit to keep it under check.

A Purpose-Driven Life as a Counter to Cheap Dopamine

The beauty of living a purpose- and goals-driven life is that most of your day will be spent in pursuing these goals. You will automatically start to withdraw from sources of cheap dopamine. If I have a writing target of say five pages a day, I structure my day around it. On the days I finish my daily target, I feel joy and satisfaction. Similarly, when I complete my workout, I feel great. Only, the joy, satisfaction and pleasure do not come from cheap dopamine, but hard effort. Now it becomes *earned* dopamine. Since cheap dopamine is kept at a minimum, my brain reward circuits work naturally, like they are supposed to. The next morning my brain automatically releases dopamine when I write or do a workout. I'm now in a positive loop, where my reward system is in sync to serve me and naturally motivate me towards accomplishing my goals. This is the massive difference between earned dopamine and cheap dopamine. Cheap dopamine pulls you away from your goals. A life of indulging in cheap dopamine highs will lead you nowhere and can even destroy you. Earned dopamine, on the other hand, will lead you to high places.

Another great thing about earned dopamine is that it doesn't lose its efficacy or cause your body and mind to develop tolerance to it. Even over time, you will continue to feel good after every workout or after every solid study session. That is the secret sauce to winning at life—find something productive that you like to do, which in turn keeps your dopamine circuits churning in a healthy, natural and effective manner, without ever losing their efficacy.

That is the secret sauce to winning at life—find something productive that you like to do, which in turn keeps your dopamine circuits churning in a healthy, natural and effective manner, without ever losing their efficacy.

The Dopamine Detox

Working single-mindedly towards your goals will automatically take you away from cheap dopamine. However, what if you are already too addicted to some form of cheap dopamine? In fact, it may even be hard for you to tell if you are addicted. You may not be aware or may be too ashamed to admit it. I can now admit that I have had all kinds of cheap dopamine addictions in the past. I still get tempted to slip up. And that is the premise of this book—to take extreme accountability. It is to become aware and admit without shame when you are screwing up.

> ❰ This is the premise of this book—to take extreme accountability. It is to become aware and admit without shame when you are screwing up. ❱

Open your phone and look at your Screentime app. Note how many hours a day you spend on the phone. It also shows you the apps you use the most. Are you spending several hours a day on Instagram or YouTube? You may have an addiction to social media content. Check what you eat all week. You could be addicted to food or sugar. Are you on adult sites three, five, seven times a week? Again, a problem. Do you look forward to meeting friends mainly because you get an excuse to drink? Are you having ten to fifteen drinks a week? All these addictions are blocking your growth. You must cut off these cheap dopamine providers. The best way to do this is through a dopamine detox—giving up the cheap dopamine activity for a significant period of time, ideally thirty days.

What you need to do is to use a gradual taper-off plan, as is done to help drug addicts cure their addiction. Aim to cut 10 to 29 per cent of the activity you are addicted to per week, until your cheap dopamine consumption is down to zero.

Smokers, drinkers or people with other addictions prefer to just go cold turkey, which means to quit completely, at one go. This could work for you too, but it will require significant mental toughness to face massive withdrawal symptoms and get through them. Things will get better, I promise.

Try not using your phone for a day or two—sounds scary, doesn't it? Perhaps gradual decrease will be better for you. For more extreme cases of food, alcohol, porn or smoking addiction, I would strongly advise consulting a doctor or addiction therapist. For most people, however, a thirty-day detox can work well to reset your brain.

Deeper Understanding of How Dopamine Works and Addiction: Lows and Peaks

It is important to understand how dopamine works in our brain to see why we end up getting addicted. Stanford University's addiction research professor, Anna

Lembke, talks about this in her book *Dopamine Nation*. Regardless of whether we are doing any dopamine-releasing activity or not, all of us have a baseline level of dopamine in our brain. This is the steady state level of this neurochemical that exists in our brain. When we do something pleasurable, dopamine levels rise, resulting in a peak over the baseline levels. Eventually, this peak subsides and the dopamine level returns to the baseline. However, each time we hit a high peak, the baseline dopamine, a few hours later, is a little lower than the earlier baseline. Imagine a container filled with water. When kept still, the level of water can be considered the baseline level. If we agitate this water, the level will rise and there will be new peaks. However, some of the water will spill out and be wasted. Hence, when the water becomes still again, the new baseline level of the water will be lower than it was at the beginning. This lower baseline level of dopamine means we will have a lower mood and feel less motivated to pursue anything.

> ❦ **Cheap dopamine chasers end up consuming more and more, even to get milder highs, and end up in an addictive loop.** ◾

To give an example, let us say we eat sugary food or drink alcohol or watch Instagram reels for an hour. We will get a dopamine high in that moment. However, invariably over time, this will be followed by a crash and a lower baseline dopamine. This is why after a night of alcohol or getting sexual release through porn, one can feel quite low or demotivated.

The brain then wants to do the activity again to stop feeling low. It wants to get another high to raise our dopamine levels. So we do it again, chase another high, get some pleasure but this also means more dopamine spills, and the eventual baseline drops even lower. Hence, we end up feeling worse. Not to mention with each subsequent use, we build tolerance and even that temporary high and the feeling of pleasure reduces too. Hence, cheap dopamine chasers end up consuming more and more, even to get milder highs, and end up in an addictive loop. This constant chasing of highs means a continuously falling baseline dopamine, which means a dwindling and permanently low level of motivation and mood over time. It can also lead to more serious conditions like depression or lack of interest in almost anything in life. This is how badly cheap dopamine fixes can destroy you. It can kill your motivation, damage pleasure and reward circuits, make you give up on your goals and eventually devastate you.

Baseline Dopamine and How to Replenish It

When baseline dopamine drops too low, it becomes extremely difficult to motivate yourself. No matter how many motivational videos you watch or books you read, it won't help. Your brain will simply not feel like working and, instead, the addict brain will keep chasing cheap dopamine highs.

Fortunately, we can fix low baseline dopamine. It's the good old dopamine detox explained earlier. Simply abstain from whatever you are addicted to for thirty days. This month of abstinence resets the dopamine system and your baseline dopamine will come back. Ensure you get good sleep in the detox period. Scientific studies have proved that good sleep helps replenish baseline dopamine.

While in this abstinence period, make yourself do things that require effort and involve discomfort. This will create the pain of genuine effort, which also helps your brain create more dopamine to compensate for it. Challenging, painful and productive activities like a strenuous workout, cold showers (not too cold!), studying for a longer period of time or making yourself do things that need to be done to achieve your goals will increase baseline dopamine.

Guarding Your Baseline Dopamine

Once your high baseline dopamine is back, guard it. You need this high baseline dopamine to stay motivated towards achieving your goals and maintain a good mood in general. Re-introduce the cheap item back in your life if you must, but with intentionality, awareness and, most importantly, moderation. A cheap dopamine fix must only be an occasional side dish in your life, never the main course. Don't live a life chasing cheap dopamine highs. They are not actually cheap. They will end up costing you a lot—maybe even your entire life.

....

Key Takeaways

- Dopamine is the neurotransmitter that motivates your brain to seek more of whatever gives you pleasure.

- Cheap dopamine is the feeling you get out of easily available things (like the feeling you get after smoking, or having junk food, or binge-watching a series).

- Cheap dopamine messes with your brain and therefore, it's important to moderate your desire for it and focus, instead, on things that really matter. With any addictive element, the magic word is moderation.

- Replace *cheap* dopamine with *earned* dopamine. Cheap dopamine addiction can be countered with a target-oriented lifestyle. Get pleasure out of achieving your life's goals like looking and feeling fit, or working towards getting a better job.

■ If you want to get rid of your addiction to cheap dopamine, stay away from it by avoiding that addictive activity for thirty days to reset your dopamine system.

....

'Look at me, I ordered pizza,' I said, 'on the day I'm telling you about cheap dopamine.'

I opened the pizza box Viraj had brought for me.

Viraj smiled. 'It's healthy pizza. Thin crust. And no cheese. I saw your order, Chetan sir. Technically it is not even pizza now,' Viraj said, 'it is bread with tomatoes on it.'

'That's true.' I said. 'It's from this new wellness place. Oh dear, what have they done to pizza?'

I took a bite of the pizza that had had its soul sucked out of it. It tasted okay. Okay is not great, but okay, I could live with it.

'I think everyone is addicted to cheap dopamine,' Viraj said.

'You are right. I am too. I finished the two ice cream cups you gave me. Didn't do the small portions. Sugar is a temptation I find hard to resist,' I said.

'All my friends are addicted too,' Viraj said, 'on their phone all the time.'

'It's a problem with the new generation. You guys have access to smartphones at this young age. We never did,' I said.

'And porn, sir. All my friends watch it too. What else can we do?'

'Meaning?'

Viraj blushed and shook his head as he smiled.

'Say it,' I said.

'We don't have girlfriends or a chance to have real sex. We still have desire,' Viraj said, saying the words 'sex' and 'desire' in a soft voice.

'Porn is the answer to that, then? Satisfies your desires or whatever?'

'It helps handle the urge, but only for a while. Makes me totally demotivated later. I don't feel like exercising, researching for other jobs, or studying. I just want to lie in bed, eat junk food and sleep.'

'Exactly. That's your baseline dopamine going lower after the porn high. And you try to lift it again by eating junk food. Which leads to another momentary high but subsequently you feel worse. Get it?'

'Yes, I get it now. Eventually this leads to a fucked-up life and becoming a fat, demotivated loser. Like me.'

'You don't have to be so harsh on yourself, Viraj.'

'It's true. Anyway, I have to get rid of my addiction to cheap dopamine. Got to earn it. Earn it with effort. It will be hard. But I will try.'

'Excellent. You learn well. See you tomorrow. I'll tell you about Rule Six.'

RULE #6

CHASE THE HARD THINGS

*'The difference between ordinary and extraordinary
is that little extra.'*

—JIMMY JOHNSON

**Life is hard. Avoiding hard things will eventually
make things harder. Better to chase the hard and
get it over with.**

Once upon a time there was a man called Bobby.
He was thirty-five years old and worked in a bank.
Bobby believed in enjoying life. He said what's the point
of living if there's no pleasure, fun or joy? It was difficult
to argue with his logic. He believed happiness came
from having fun. He ate everything he wanted to—chole
bhature, potato chips, gulab jamuns, ice creams, butter
chicken and whatever else he found tasty. Food gave him
real happiness. He drank like a fish. He loved his whisky.
He became an expert at identifying different flavours

and tastes of various single malts. Every day, he ate and drank well. He felt he was living his life to the fullest. The key to happiness, he believed, was in chasing pleasure and avoiding pain. He never bothered to exercise. He had a comfortable sofa and a large flat-screen TV. Every evening, he came back from his bank job and settled on the couch in front of his TV. He poured himself a glass of fine whisky with ice. He served himself a plate of fried, salty and crispy snacks to munch on while he watched his favourite show.

'Ah,' he would exclaim, leaning back on his sofa, 'this is life. This is happiness.'

Sure enough, many people agreed with him. People used to cite Bobby's example to describe a person who totally enjoys his life. He doesn't take tension. He doesn't make life difficult. He doesn't let stupid things like his body's shape bother him. Bobby is an example of how life should be lived, they said.

Time went by. Bobby turned forty. His belly expanded. He had gained 20 kilograms in five years. It didn't matter to Bobby. He just bought clothes a few sizes larger—he went from L to XXL. His friends told him his big frame suited his big personality—that of a jovial man who loves life. Bobby would eat and drink lavishly, alone after a long day of work and with his friends on the weekend.

More time passed. Bobby turned fifty. In the ten years that had passed, a few things had changed. Bobby had fallen sick a few times. His doctor told him he had hypertension and diabetes. However, this was common at this age. Millions of Indian men of that age have diabetes or hypertension or both. Hence, Bobby wasn't alone. His doctor also told him that at 120 kilograms, he was 40 kilograms, overweight.

'What to do, I love my food,' Bobby said and laughed.

The doctor gave Bobby half a dozen medicines to control his blood pressure, blood sugar, cholesterol and other vital markers.

Bobby felt fortunate to have a good doctor who could cure all his ailments. He came home, back to the same life.

Two years later, at fifty-two, Bobby had a heart attack and died. His friends cried. They missed their friend who 'lived life to the fullest' and 'on his own terms' and was 'happy'. Then the friends went back home to their own lives. That was the end of Bobby's story.

Unfortunately, such stories are extremely common these days. Bobby, or people like him, think that the path to a happy life is simple. It is to chase pleasure and avoid discomfort. This would lead to a life filled with pleasure and devoid of pain. Voila, that is a happy life!

Except, they are wrong. You now know how dopamine works in your brain. Cheap dopamine pleasures merely give temporary dopamine highs. They only agitate the existing dopamine, which is inevitably followed by a crash and even lower baseline dopamine levels. The only way to generate or create dopamine is to put in significant effort,

❮ A happy, fulfilled and motivated life isn't about chasing pleasure and comfort. It is, instead, about chasing the right effort and discomfort. ❯

take the pain and do things that give you discomfort. Then, to compensate or make things bearable, the brain creates new dopamine.

Hence, a happy, fulfilled and motivated life isn't about chasing pleasure and comfort. It is, instead, about chasing the right effort and discomfort.

Did Bobby truly live a happy life? That depends on how you define 'a happy life'. Some may say he lived less, but when he lived he made the most of it. But let's examine Bobby's 'happy life' in a little more detail.

First, his life could have been longer. He could have lived to, say, eighty-five. He died at fifty-two, which means he died thirty-three years before the end of his potential life. Does being dead sound happy to you? Even of the fifty-two years he lived, he started developing ailments in his early forties. His weight meant he had little energy to walk, his sleep suffered and he did not look and feel as good as he could have. Sure, he drank the most expensive alcohol and ate the tastiest food. However, at the end of the day it was just the high-chasing, eventually crashing cheap dopamine. Over time, neither the food nor the alcohol gave him as much pleasure as it once had.

Chasing Hard Things

Don't be like Bobby. Don't avoid hard things. In fact, to get ahead and to be happy in life, you must actively chase hard things. Real achievement is hard. It is tough to study for years and clear an entrance exam. It is difficult to be consistent with your diet and exercise over a period of time. It takes a lot to keep going after getting rejected for a job. It is challenging to start a business. All of this is indeed very, very hard.

But let me tell you what else is hard. It is hard to see yourself fail at that entrance exam because you did not study. It is hard to be fat. It is hard to be unattractive. It is tough to work at a mediocre job day after day. It is difficult knowing you will never succeed in making a class jump. It is hard to always feel like a loser and remain demotivated. It is hard to always want, but never taste real success in life. It is hard to be sick, unhealthy and get heart attacks. These are all the 'hards' you will have to face if you avoid the 'hards' of doing the work you need to do.

Here's a simple quote that is one of my favourites. It's just three words.

Life is uphill

That's it. The moment you understand this simple and beautiful concept, everything becomes easier. Life is fundamentally a struggle. Life is a beautiful, huge green hill. It is beautiful but you also need to climb the hill to really make the most of it. You must hike up a bit every

> **Every day, wake up and realize that you have to climb uphill. Do something hard every day.**

day. If you avoid this hike, because it is too much effort, you will stop growing. More likely, you will slip down.

Every day, wake up and realize that you have to climb uphill. Do something hard every day. It could be gruelling physical or mental effort. It could be the hard task of avoiding temptation or laziness. It could be the hard process of facing rejection. All of this has to be there in your life on a regular basis. If you don't chase your hard each day, the hard will chase you down one day. By then

> **If you don't chase your hard each day, the hard will chase you down one day.**

it will be too late. You can't resurrect a failed career in your fifties, or undo a heart attack. Looking back, it would have been much easier to do a bit of

hard work every day when you could. Life is an uphill climb, and there is beauty even in this effort.

What about Fun and Pleasure?

Does chasing hard mean one never goes after sheer pleasure? How about having fun for fun's sake? Should one never have an ice cream, make love or have a drink with friends? Should one never go dancing, watch a movie, chill on their phone? Can I never laze around in bed?

No, chasing the hard doesn't mean a zero-fun life. It means to go after the hard and tackle it first. You first chase your hard, get your uphill climb done with for the day, week or month and enjoy yourself after that. Take a break at the end of the day. Do whatever relaxes you. Take a longer break after a few months. Maybe go on a vacation. Have an ice cream now and then. But make sure it is only now and then, or on rare occasions. What you don't want is a life of chasing pleasure. That is, chasing cheap highs, falling baseline dopamine tolerance, addiction, low motivation, depression, eventual failure and unhappiness. Occasional pleasures, whether it is the small highs of tasty food, watching a movie or listening to music are fine. These things can't become the focus of your life, that's all.

> No, chasing the hard doesn't mean a zero-fun life. It means to go after the hard and tackle it first. You first chase your hard, get your uphill climb done with for the day, week or month and enjoy yourself after that.

Once you realize that effort is good for you, chasing the hard will come more naturally. You won't even need a motivational speaker, video or book. Your own wonderful brain will generate all the motivation you need. Just chase that hard, do your daily climb and make the most of this steep but wonderful hill called life.

Key Takeaways

- A joyful and motivated life isn't about chasing pleasure and comfort; it is about chasing the right effort and discomfort.

- Don't avoid hard things; instead, chase them to make your grand visions and dreams come true.

- It's difficult to achieve big goals. But it's more difficult to see yourself failing at achieving them.

- If you don't chase your hard each day, the hard will chase you down one day.

....

'I implemented what you told me yesterday. I chased my hard. Today, I woke up at 5 a.m. I ran 5 kilometres. Then I came back and worked on my LinkedIn Profile. Only then did I start my food deliveries,' Viraj said.

He had come in the morning to my house. I had ordered breakfast, taking a break from my intermittent fasting.

'That's great, Viraj. You are changing. That's good.'

I opened the food packet. It had hot oatmeal in a glass jar.

'I will never seek the soft life again,' Viraj said. He held the sides of his stomach. 'And I don't even want to be soft anymore. I want to chase hard, get fit.'

'You will. Follow the rules sincerely and you'll be surprised to see where life takes you.'

'What's today's rule?'

'Come, let's eat the elephant.'

'What?'

'That's the next rule. Eat the elephant,' I said, eating a spoonful of my oatmeal.

RULE #7

EAT THE ELEPHANT

*'The journey of a thousand miles begins with
a single step.'*

—LAO TZU

**Achieving anything remarkable always requires
long-term effort.**

Here's a question for you. How will you eat an
elephant?

This isn't one of those trick questions. I'm serious—
how will you eat an elephant?

You may answer that you can't. Elephants are massive.
Even the smaller Asian elephants we see in India weigh
between 2,000 and 5,000 kilograms. Hence, at an average
weight of 3,500 kilograms, it would seem impossible for
a human being to eat an elephant.

But let us approach this problem differently. We
humans eat around 1.5 kilograms of food each day (a
lot, isn't it?). If an elephant weighs 3,500 kilograms,
you could eat one in 3,500/1.5 = 2,333 days, or around

6.5 years. Hence, one answer to this question could be: 'You can eat an elephant by cutting it into little pieces, and eating it over many years.'

Similarly, the most difficult, insurmountable tasks in life can be dealt with effectively by breaking them down or cutting them up into small pieces.

How you cut your big problem into tiny pieces, and work on eating or finishing up those tiny pieces one at a time determines your success in life. That's one of the secrets to life—learning to eat your elephant. It takes a long time. It's monotonous and can be boring as hell. It requires determination, focus and sidelining your own pleasure. After all, who wants to eat an elephant, and only an elephant, day after day? However, this is the one tool available to a person without money, privilege and connections. If you can grind away at achieving your goal and keep at it, get bored but still do it day after day, then you can achieve a lot. That's how I did it, despite not being particularly gifted or a genius.

Here are some elephants I have eaten in my life, which I'm sharing with you to explain the concept better.

> ❝ The most difficult, insurmountable tasks in life can be dealt with effectively by breaking them down or cutting up the task into small pieces. ❞

> ❝ If you can grind away at achieving your goal and keep at it, get bored but still do it day after day, then you can achieve a lot. ❞

My First Elephant: IIT

I was not an extraordinary student in school. I never topped my class. My teachers didn't refer to me as 'IIT material'. I ranked in the teens in a class of fifty students. My teachers used to describe me as 'clever but distracted' or 'above average' at best. I was never 'exceptional'. That's how everyone saw me—and I did too.

I studied at Army Public School in New Delhi. My father, who was in the Army, was often posted in different cities. However, my mother held a government job in Delhi and we kids lived with her. My younger brother and I did our entire schooling from Army Public School. It's a huge school, accommodating mostly Army kids from all over the country. Sections in many grades ran from A, B, C all the way to Z. In such a massive school, it is hard to have high academic rigour. The school was good at one thing though—there was always opportunity for the students to have fun! It was one of the most enjoyable phases of my life. School was, for the most part, a big party for me.

The most popular choice for what my classmates wanted to do after school was join the Army. Out of our class of 300, only five students and I were aiming to appear for the IIT-JEE exam.

At home, too, I didn't have a particularly conducive environment to study for IIT. My father was away a fair bit, and when he was in town, things would be tense at home. As I mentioned earlier, my parents had frequent arguments. Somehow, I always fell short of what my father wanted me to be. I wasn't sporty enough, disciplined enough or respectful enough. Maybe he expected me to be like an obedient army soldier. He would frequently yell and at times beat me, yes, even with a belt occasionally. And if this wasn't enough, there was a neighbour, a boy who was four years older than me. I don't recollect how it started, but when I was eleven, he would undress me and perform certain acts I had little idea about. They seemed somewhat wrong and shameful to my young mind, but at the same time there was something secretive and pleasurable about it as well. Maybe I was too innocent to figure it all out. Ask anyone who has had such incidents happen to them, and you'll find they are confused about what it all meant to them when it happened. That boy introduced me to sexual activity, and at that point I didn't know what to make of it. It was an occasional activity done in the afternoon to distract myself, perhaps from all the domestic mayhem around me.

As you can see, my home wasn't exactly a nurturing environment for a star to flourish. In fact, looking back, I realize what I went through was horrifying and traumatic. However, at that moment I didn't think so. I felt this is how every home is supposed to be. This is the life of every child. I remember I would be busy solving IIT-JEE physics numericals, and then my father's dreaded voice would call out to me. I would immediately wonder what was in store for me this time: a yelling, a beating, a belt? Maybe all three.

I was in terrible circumstances. And yet, or maybe that's exactly why, I decided to prepare for IIT. I had to get out of this misery. IIT seemed to be the only ticket out that appeared to be within my reach. I just had to study hard to get there. However, I didn't initially realize how difficult it would be to clear the entrance exam. Nobody in my entire extended family, nor in my neighbourhood, had ever cleared this test. It required a long, rigorous preparation, a thorough understanding of scientific concepts and thousands of hours of hard work. It really was like eating an elephant. I had no guidance on how to prepare for it.

Yet, I was determined to go for it.

Step 1: Identifying the Elephant Cuts

The first step for me was to see the IIT-JEE elephant in its entirety and figure out how to chop it into little pieces. During my time, there was only one IIT Joint Entrance Exam or JEE (today there are the IIT-JEE Mains and the IIT-JEE Advanced). The exam I took had three tests—Physics, Chemistry and Maths. Hence, I understood how to make the first three cuts of my IIT elephant—Physics, Chemistry and Maths.

Next, I went through the syllabus in each subject. Mathematics ranged from calculus, trigonometry, algebra, matrices, probability and around thirty other topics. Physics and Chemistry had forty-odd topics each. It was scary, just as it would be when you see a huge elephant and realize you must eat it all. However, I at least had some cut points. My IIT elephant was cut like the figure below.

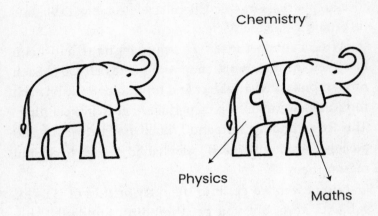

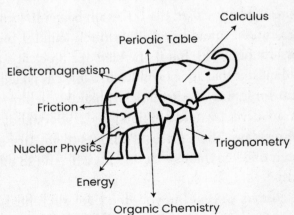

CUTTING THE IIT ELEPHANT

Cut level 1: Physics—Chemistry—Maths.

Cut level 2: Physics—Electromagnetism, Friction, Nuclear Physics, Energy and 36 others.

Maths—Calculus, Trigonometry and 38 others

Chemistry—Organic Chemistry, Periodic Table and 38 others

After I made these cuts, my elephant had been chopped up into more than 100 pieces already. Each piece represented a subject and topic. Now, within each topic there were sub-topics, perhaps four to five per topic. This led to another cut, and I finally had before me 500 pieces of the monstrous IIT elephant. I needed to eat and master them all.

I don't want to get into the nitty-gritties of IIT-JEE subjects here, but you get the point. Suddenly, this massive elephant called the IIT exam began to look like a Lego model made up of 500, much smaller blocks. That's a lot of blocks, but if I tackled one block at a time, I could master that specific block in a few days. Hence, if the sub-topic was Mathematics/Integral Calculus/Area under a Curve, I would attain a good understanding of it in three days. Then, I had 499 blocks to go. That's still a lot, but one less than 500, I told myself. And so on and so forth.

Of course, in real life you don't get such neat cuts by topic. You may also have to tackle several blocks at the same time. Even for IIT, I would study some Maths,

Physics and Chemistry daily, and cover several topics on each day. However, the principle is the same—attaining big goals by breaking the effort down into little parts.

Step 2: Eating the Cuts, One Piece at a Time

Once I had cut the IIT elephant into smaller chunks, it came down to keeping at it. Slowly, daily, I ate a bit of the elephant. I had 500 pieces and two years to eat them all up. I studied five hours a day, five days a week, for the exam. Five hours of studying a day may not seem like a lot, but when done consistently over time it can work miracles. During my time, IIT preparation involved joining correspondence classes. The concept of online coaching did not exist then. No rockstar, glamorous teachers. I received packets of study material every month via physical mail. Slowly, I ate the elephant. I enjoyed it on some days and hated it on others. Sometimes, I slipped. My motivation levels dropped. I quit preparing for weeks. However, I always manage to pull myself back. I kept at it for two years. IIT entrance prep is extremely challenging. The hardest part of the IIT-JEE prep isn't Physics, Chemistry or Maths. It's the keeping at it, the consistent putting in of effort—in other words, it is eating the elephant that is most difficult. This ultimately decides whether you make it or not.

Two years later, I gave the IIT entrance exam. The results came out after three months.

On the day the results were to be announced, I took a DTC bus to the IIT campus in Delhi. The results were stuck on the institute's boundary walls. Next to my roll number, it said 'All India Rank 326'. I was numb for a full ten seconds before I realized I had cracked it and made it to IIT. My elephant-eating method had paid off. And I entered the college of my dreams. That ultimately changed my life.

My Second Elephant: The First Book

I'm going to skip telling you about the IIM entrance exam elephant (the CAT) as that journey was similar to preparing for IIT. Instead, let me tell you about the next elephant in my life—my first book.

I always had an interest in writing. I would submit articles, short stories and essays to the school and IIT magazines. I would write plays and skits. I was good but, again, not exceptional. People would read my stuff and enjoy it. However, nobody ever said I had massive potential as a writer. Nor did I think so. And never did I imagine I could write a full book.

'An entire book! No way. That's for intellectuals and literature majors. I'm a mechanical engineer and MBA. I work in a bank,' I used to say in my head. Yet, despite being too scared to try my hand at it, I had a desire to be an author.

I was working at a bank in Hong Kong when, one day, on a walk back home after work, I had a mental conversation with myself.

'What is stopping me from writing a book?' I asked myself.

'Because it is scary,' another voice in my head replied.

'What is scary?' I countered.

'It's a big project. Hundreds of pages of writing. It's not an article I can finish in one day. It could take months, or even years. I have never done this before, and the fear makes me freeze.'

'But basically it's another elephant. It's scary because you must eat the huge elephant.'

'Well, yes.'

'And how do you eat an elephant?'

'By cutting it into smaller pieces. Then eating one piece at a time, over a long time.'

'Bingo. There you go. You now know what to do.'

I had found my next big elephant. After the IIT-JEE, it was now my first novel. (Incidentally, my first book was also a story about my IIT days.) I thought if I wrote one page a day, I would have 365 pages in a year. One year seemed like a long time. However, if I just focused on that one page for that day, it would be like writing an article. I had written articles before. Of course, I would have to plan the book and make an outline. In other words, I would have to first make the various cuts of the book elephant. It took me a month to make the writing plan. After that, I had to eat that elephant, one piece at a time, or one page a day, every day. For an entire year.

It wasn't easy. This elephant eating didn't go as planned either. I had a busy job at an investment bank. Hence, it became a struggle to do that one page a day. I modified the plan to two pages a day on the weekends, and then one page a day on three of the five workdays. This allowed me some off days from writing when my bank work became too busy. Even then, it took me two years instead of the planned one year to complete the first draft. Of course, this was only the first draft, which is usually terrible.

I had to edit this draft, which is another elephant-eating exercise. I did a few rounds of editing and finished the book. Happy ending? Not yet. I submitted the book to publishers. All of whom rejected it point-blank.

Now it was time to eat one more elephant. I had to rewrite the entire book. Three years and several elephants later, I finally had a publisher accept my book. The rest, as they say, is history. My first book, titled *Five Point Someone*, became a mega bestseller. It sold more copies in India than almost any other English novel had until then. This book was also adapted for screen as *3 Idiots*, a blockbuster movie. The three elephants that I had eaten— writing the first draft, editing the book and rewriting the entire book—changed my entire career and my life.

My Other Elephants

I have eaten many other elephants in my life. I won't elaborate on them, but some of them include making the rounds to get a break in Bollywood, establishing myself as a newspaper columnist by writing hundreds of columns over several years, writing screenplays and losing weight for better health.

These are all different goals, or different elephants. They all seem difficult and insurmountable at first. However, the process of tackling them is the same—you look at the elephant, find the cut points, divide up the whole into little pieces and work on eating one piece at a time over a long period of time.

I'm neither a gifted genius nor do I have extraordinary talent. Fortunately, I'm aware of it. I make up for this deficiency by doing what most people find unpalatable to do, which is eating the elephant. Sometimes I succeed, while other times I fail. However, it only takes a few big successes to make a successful life. Eating elephants is hard, but you only need to eat a few of them in your life. One entrance exam, one successful business, one hit book, one great promotion or job offer can put your life in a different orbit. Eating elephants, no matter how unsavoury, is the best way for common people to make that class jump.

> Eating elephants, no matter how unsavoury, is the best way for common people to make that class jump.

Identifying Your Elephant

Some people have a clear idea about their goals in life. They want to become a lawyer, a civil servant, a doctor, an engineer, an MBA or a chartered accountant. Many Indian students are in this zone. In such cases, the elephant is staring right at you. If you want to be a doctor, you need to get admission into a good medical college. That usually requires massive amounts of preparation for an entrance exam. That's your medical exam elephant. Ditto for the entrance exams for other professions. If you are a student, doing well in your academics is your elephant. Your fitness, Rule One in this book, is another elephant. If you have a business, are learning a language, perfecting a skill, mastering coding or a musical instrument, all these are goals that require eating the respective elephants. It is not the easiest thing to do, so you can only eat one or two elephants at a time. Usually, it will be your main career goal and your fitness. Just eating these two elephants will take a lot out of you. I have eaten many elephants in life, but usually tackled only one elephant at a time. I

❦ Find your one big, juicy elephant. Don't be scared by its size. Break it down into hundreds of little pieces. Eat a single piece at a time, over months and years. Enjoy the adventure. Stick to it, and you will get done eventually. Success will inevitably come your way. ❧

couldn't have prepared for IIT and written my first book simultaneously.

Find your one big, juicy elephant. Don't be scared by its size. Break it down into hundreds of little pieces. Eat a single piece at a time, over months and years. Enjoy the adventure. Stick to it, and you will get done eventually. Success will inevitably come your way. Everyone around you will be shocked and amazed at how you did it. Some will call you superhuman and a genius. Whereas all you did was, piece by piece, eat your big elephant.

The Psychology behind Eating the Elephant

Humans are unique creatures in the animal kingdom. We are the only ones with the ability to plan and prepare for the future. We can understand we have an entrance exam we have to do well in after one year. We can then make a study plan. Cows and monkeys can't do that. They can only think about that moment or day. Cows can't think ahead and learn to grow their own grass. Monkeys can't build houses to protect themselves from rain. We can. However, we have evolved from animals. Around 99 per cent of our DNA is the same as that of chimpanzees. We still find plans, vision and long-term effort challenging and scary. We, like our animal ancestors, are pretty good at short-term tasks. To give an example, a chimpanzee will climb up banana trees and bring down bunches. This is a short-term effort. Similarly, if I tell you to clean your room, something that may take you half an hour, most of you will have no problem doing it. If I tell you to go buy vegetables from the market, you can do it without an issue. If you had to only study one chapter of trigonometry, and finish the twenty problems at the end of it, you would be less daunted by the task. You could complete that assignment today itself. It only requires short-term effort. However, if I tell you to prepare for the IIT-JEE, it will scare you. Humans are good at short-term effort. We suck at long-term effort.

> ❝Achieving anything remarkable always requires long-term effort.❞

Achieving anything remarkable always requires long-term effort. Short-term effort is never considered great. Nobody will tell you, 'Wow, what a guy, he cleaned his room.' Or 'Oh, how amazing! He bought 3 kilograms of tomatoes from the market today!' The world will recognize you when you achieve something big. Cracking an entrance exam, transforming your body, winning a sports championship—all require long-term effort.

The trick is to cut this long-term effort into less scary, psychologically manageable, small, daily, short-term pieces. Work on these pieces, eat the elephant one bite at a time, and eventually it will all add up and lead to massive success.

Key Takeaways

- Anyone who has achieved anything worthwhile in life has eaten an elephant, i.e., worked for a long time on something consistently, by cutting something big and intimidating into small pieces.

- Don't feel intimidated by 'elephants' or big goals. Divide your big goal into many tiny goals and target each of them one at a time.

- Tackle only one or a maximum of two 'elephants' at a time, because big life goals come after long-term effort.

- After identifying your goal or 'elephant', step 1 is to decide the cuts of the elephant—in what parts do you want to divide your big goal into.

- Step 2 involves sub-dividing these parts into smaller parts in order to make them even more easily achievable. Then you can go about handling one part at a time.

....

Viraj bit his lower lip. His eyes stared into infinity. He seemed deep in thought. I finished my oatmeal.

'Are you with me?' I said.

'Huh? Yes.'

'Did you listen to what I said?'

'I haven't eaten ...'

'What? You should have told me. We could have shared my meal. I have more food in the fridge. Should I bring you something?'

Viraj shook his head.

'No, not that. I haven't eaten my elephant. Actually, I haven't even eaten a goat or a rabbit.'

'What?' I said.

'I was an average student in school. I believed I was meant to be this way. Never aimed for high marks. Never tried for a good college. I didn't even work on my body. I found Arpita. She liked me. I felt she was enough, that's all I needed. She was the source of happiness in my life.'

'No one person can be that. It isn't even fair to them.'

'I didn't know that. I spent so much time trying to impress Arpita, to keep her around, to ensure she was happy and wouldn't leave me. In that time, I could have done so much with my life,' Viraj said, and bit his lip again to prevent himself from crying.

'In that time you could have eaten an elephant?'

'Definitely. I could have cleared the entrance exam for a government job in the railways. My friend did. He asked me to prepare with him. I didn't.'

'Why not?'

'It seemed hard. Too much work. I thought I'm an average student. I can't do it. Plus, it would have meant less time with Arpita, my only source of joy.'

'So, you never gave it a shot?'

'No. I didn't even appear for the exam. I feel so ashamed now.'

A tear fell from Viraj's left eye. He wiped it with his hands.

'There's always another elephant to eat, Viraj.'

Viraj looked at me.

I continued. 'There are a lot of difficult things you could still do. Elephants you can eat that can change your life for the better. If you are ready to do the work.'

'I am ready. What's my new elephant?'

'Only you can figure that out. Take your time. Think about it.'

Viraj nodded. He stood up to leave.

'Was it difficult?' Viraj asked. 'Sharing all that?'

'Sharing what?'

'The stuff that your neighbour did to you.'

'It was one of hardest things for me to share, yes. To deal with all the shame,' I spoke slowly. 'But I had to do it. Now that I have shared it, it has unburdened me. Besides, I can't tell you to do hard things but not do them myself.'

'Why do you feel shame? You were eleven.'

'I don't know.'

'It wasn't right, what happened to you.'

I nodded. Viraj came forward and gave me a reassuring hug. I smiled, fighting back tears.

'You okay?' Viraj asked.

'I'm okay, yes. Thank you. I just realized something.'

'What?'

'I need these sessions as much as you need them. It helps me sort out my past.'

'I'm glad. And I definitely need them. I will see you tomorrow?'

'Yes, today was elephant. Tomorrow, cockroach.'

'What? Cockroach?' Viraj said with a surprised expression.

'Tomorrow.' I smiled, waving him goodbye.

RULE #8

BE THE COCKROACH

'In nature, it is not the strongest or most intelligent that survives, but it is the most adaptive that does.'

—CHARLES DARWIN

Adapt with the changing times, situations and the opportunity on hand. Only those who adapt survive.

What feelings does a cockroach invoke in you? Disgust? Do you think they are yuck? Ugly, horrible, cringe-inducing insects? You aren't alone. Nobody likes or respects cockroaches. However, I will make you look at this creature differently. It is a creature which is my role model. Maybe after reading this chapter, it will be yours too.

A cockroach as a role model? Aren't role models supposed to be more like strong tigers and fearless lions? Or the majestic eagle or hawk? Why a cockroach? It is even used as a derogatory term.

I will tell you why I admire the cockroach. It is because of the one amazing quality they have. Cockroaches are amongst the most adaptive creatures on earth.

The ability to adapt is extremely important in life. Those who can adapt continue to grow. Those who can't get stuck and decline. This isn't just my theory or opinion. This is an observation from nature. Let's look again at the quote at the start of this chapter from Charles Darwin:

'In nature, it is not the strongest or most intelligent that survives, but it is the most adaptive that does.'

Charles Darwin wasn't a motivational guru, business leader or life coach. He was an evolutionary biologist. He spent his life on remote islands, studying wildlife and nature.

He made an extraordinary observation. Nature doesn't care how intelligent, or strong you are. If you don't adapt, which means to change according to the needs of time, you will perish. Let's take an example. Millions of years ago, there were large animals called dinosaurs. Some of these creatures were the biggest animals on earth, far larger than elephants. Nobody could mess with them. They ruled the world. Then, the ice started melting, tectonic plates shifted and other natural changes occurred. The dinosaurs couldn't adjust to the new environment. Eventually, they became extinct. Today, you only see fake ones in movies with special effects.

❝The ability to adapt is extremely important in life. Those who can adapt continue to grow.❞

Cockroaches also existed millions of years ago. They were there then; they are there now. Today, they don't merely exist, they thrive. You will find them everywhere—in kitchens, bathrooms, cars, restaurants, offices, airports and just about everywhere else. That's because cockroaches can adapt and live anywhere. When their environment changes, they don't freak out and worry. They are chill about change. That's what an adaptive attitude is all about—*chill about change*. With any change in their surroundings, I imagine they just shrug and say, 'The world is changing, but it's fine, we will change too.' Or, 'Okay, we used to live in the jungle, now we have to live in Gurgaon. It's okay, we will adjust!' Or, 'We used to eat leaves and insects, now we have to eat cereal. It's okay, we will adjust!'

This *'It's okay, we will adjust!'* said with a smile is the attitude that gets you far in life. Most people find it hard to adjust or change. Cockroaches don't worry about it.

> This *"It's okay, we will adjust!"* said with a smile is the attitude that gets you far in life.

A good way to check how a species is doing is to see if they are reproducing well. Cockroaches breed prolifically. You will find their eggs under sofa cushions, in cupboard crevices, in corners of the kitchen, in the bathroom and even in your car. Summer, monsoon or winter. Hot or cold. Cockroaches continue to multiply wherever they are. Think about this—multinational companies, brands like Baygon and HIT, are in the business of killing cockroaches. They have factories and offices, and manufacturing, HR and accounting departments. All working towards one goal—to kill cockroaches in this world. When an employee of their company goes to work, I imagine their kids asking them, 'Dad/Mom, where are you going?'

'I'm going to office,' they reply.

'What are you going to office to do?'

'We are trying to kill off all cockroaches.'

Well, have they been able to? No. Despite the capital, resources and people put on the job to eliminate cockroaches, we haven't been able to get rid of them. The government doesn't protect cockroaches like it does tigers (who have been reduced to a tiny number, by the way). No society or club exists to protect cockroaches, like they do to protect dolphins and elephants. Nobody likes cockroaches, everyone wants to kill them and, yet, the humble cockroach survives on this planet, undefeated by humans. They have even adapted themselves to the bug spray. Studies have shown their blood can adjust to the spray so that the latter is no longer toxic. It's almost like a glass of beer for them after a while. In an era where so

> No society or club exists to protect cockroaches, like they do to protect dolphins and elephants. Nobody likes cockroaches, everyone wants to kill them and, yet, the humble cockroach survives on this planet, undefeated by humans.

many majestic and beautiful animal species are becoming extinct, our friend the cockroach has no such issues.

Now do you see the cockroach differently? Do you have newfound respect for this pretty cool creature who can also teach you something?

Applying the Cockroach Attitude to My Life in School

One disadvantage of being in a school for Army kids is that you or your friends have to part company after a few years. It is heartbreaking to have your best friend in class VI leave in class VIII, but such is Army life. Invariably, your dad gets posted to a new Army town, and the family follows. I didn't have to change schools as my mother worked in Delhi and looked after my brother and me. However, many of my classmates left every year and were replaced with new arrivals, Army kids who had just shifted to Delhi. It sucked to have your close friends leave. This was the pre-internet era. Friends leaving meant they were gone. There were no emails, no WhatsApp texts or video calls via which to stay in touch. Invariably, we had to learn to make new friends and bond with the new arrivals. I feel that this peculiar aspect of Army culture developed my ability to adapt better than many others. Most Army kids learn to adapt well. They have good social skills and can fit in anywhere quickly, which in turn helps them do well in life.

Not only did I have to learn to make new friends every few years, I also had to adapt to the traumatic situation at home. How are you to study if you constantly see your parents fight? Well, what would a cockroach do? It wouldn't lament its doomed fate, for sure. A cockroach wouldn't say, 'I can't study in this terrible situation, which is not my fault.' Rather, a cockroach would figure out a way. It would say, 'Oh gosh! This noise! I better find some cotton wool for my ears.' That's exactly what I did. I stuffed cotton balls into my ears and studied. I listened to music on a cheap Walkman to drown out the constant arguments. I told myself: 'These books I'm studying will get me out of this miserable place.' I didn't say, 'I *can't* study because of the situation at home.' I said, 'I *have* to study because of the situation at home.' In doing this, I adapted. I changed the narrative of my life to one that pushed me in a productive direction. The atmosphere at home became a propellant for me, an edge or advantage that other students did not have. I almost felt fortunate to come from a disturbed home. Otherwise, if everything was amazing and comfortable, why would I push myself to work so hard?

Applying the Cockroach Attitude to My Career

Career Adaptation: Banking

My entire career strategy, which has by no means been perfect, can be described in two words: constant adaptation. My first job was with an American investment bank in Hong Kong. I got the job straight out of campus in IIM Ahmedabad, and I never gave much thought to the culture shock waiting for me.

It was my first time being out of India. The Chinese culture of Hong Kong and the American culture in the bank came as a jolt. Chinese food in Hong Kong isn't the same as the Indianized Chinese food back home. It is bland and just a lot of meat. Chinese people can seem just as bland at first, as they largely ignore you on the streets.

In office, I found Americans had a certain way of doing business. They can be extremely friendly outside office hours. However, they are completely dry and task-oriented at work. They also have their own principles about personal space, political correctness and which topics of conversation may be too personal. It was confusing for an FOB (fresh-of-the-boat) Indian like me.

In the initial few months, all my college batchmates who had come to work in Hong Kong from India felt alienated and lonely. We huddled together and longed for home. We hunted for the rare Indian restaurants where we could get daal and rice. None of us liked Hong Kong or working in an American bank. One night, I realized this wasn't going to

❡ If I kept hankering for India in Hong Kong, or expecting Americans to behave like Indians, I would be disappointed forever. I then did what the cockroach would do—adapt, and say, "It's okay! We will adjust!" ❡

work. Hong Kong was my life now. If I kept hankering for India in Hong Kong, or expecting Americans to behave like Indians, I would be disappointed forever. I then did what the cockroach would do—adapt, and say, 'It's okay! We will adjust!'

I stopped hunting for Indian restaurants and switched to local cuisine. Chinese food didn't taste good at all for a few weeks. Eventually, my taste buds adjusted. I bought a book on American culture. Americans are the opposite of Indian mothers. They will never ask questions on how much you earn or why you aren't married yet! I learnt about American values and norms, such as individuality and independence, not saying anything that would seem too judgemental or invasive of someone's personal space. I tried to enjoy Hong Kong and my job for what it had to offer. I realized the city is indeed beautiful and efficient. It has mountains, beaches and country parks. You can hike on desolate nature trails and party in buzzy areas at night. I also discovered Chinese food has variety, just as India has different food from different regions. Some regional Chinese food dishes taste really good too (Indians, in particular, like the spicier cuisine of Sichuan, which is a province in China). I also managed to make a close set of American friends (as close as Americans can be, that is, since nobody is into each other like us desis). These adaptations made my life in Hong Kong much better. They also helped me survive banking in an alien city for over a decade.

Career Adaptation: Writing

I worked at Goldman Sachs, one of the most famous investment banks in the world. My job paid me in dollars. Yet, I felt something missing from my life. That's the reason I decided to write a book. I ate the elephant and finished my first book while still working at the bank. After that, I submitted it to several publishers. All of them rejected it. Most of them did not even bother to explain why. In my regular job, I was an international investment banker. In the publishing world in India, I was a struggling nobody. At that time the names that mattered in English-language publishing were Arundhati Roy and Vikram Seth. They had both been recognized in the West and had won multiple prizes there. I was neither known nor did I write like them. My book was about three friends in IIT, who drink, smoke weed and goof around in college. One of them dates a professor's daughter and makes out with her on the terrace of the IIT academic building. No Western jury was going to give my book a prize. That's why Indian publishers had zero interest in my book.

One rejection came, then another and yet another. I had submitted the book to ten publishers. Nine said no in a row. The tenth said no too. However, they gave me a few reasons why the book did not work in its present form. For the two years of work I had put into writing the book, I had ten rejections to show. This wasn't easy to deal with. 'I am an investment banker at Goldman Sachs! I went to IIT and IIM. How can you all reject me? Are you guys stupid?' I wanted to scream at them. I couldn't. It wouldn't have helped anyway.

Finally, this is the question that helped: *What would a cockroach do?*

A cockroach wouldn't scream if it was chased out of the kitchen. It would simply hide under the shelves, wait for an appropriate time and return. If chased again, it would maybe move to another room or house. It would adapt. I realized I would have to as well. I would have to set aside my ego and get off my high horse about being an IITian, a banker and whatever else I had been until then. In the publishing world, I was nothing. My book was one of the hundreds of manuscripts publishers had on their desks every month. Each wannabe writer thinks they have written the next masterpiece. Publishers didn't care if I had worked on it for two years or twenty, how personal the story was or how surely I thought it would work. They cared about what their evaluation committee thought of it.

I swallowed my pride and tried calling the publishers again. Most didn't take my calls. The tenth publisher, the one who had given me the reason for rejection did answer my call. I asked them for a meeting. They seemed reluctant. I tried again. They said no. I asked them if there was anyone else whom I could speak to who could give me brutal feedback on my book. They suggested one of their published writers, a lady named Shinie Antony, who could give me more detailed feedback. I sent my manuscript to Shinie in Delhi. She read it and told me nothing really worked in the book. However, she saw some sparks of humour in the writing.

'Write a funny book,' Shinie said to me.

'Make it more gripping,' the tenth publisher who had rejected me told me, when I kept pushing them for more feedback.

I decided to do both—write a funny *and* gripping book. It meant a full rewrite, a literal pressing of the delete button on two years of work. I did it. I ate the elephant again, this time having adapted to the feedback. One year later, I had another book.

I sent the rewrite to Shinie and she took it to the tenth publisher. Both of them liked it. The publisher was Rupa & Company, and they agreed to publish *Five Point Someone*. I published nine books with Rupa over the next twelve years, each of which became a major bestseller. It has been twenty years since I met Shinie. She still helps edit my books and is the first reader of every one of them. She is also the first person I mention in the acknowledgements for every book. (Including this one. Hello to you, Shinie, as you read this during the edits.)

I sometimes think of the what-ifs. What if I didn't adapt and rewrite the book? What if I thought all the publishers rejecting me were losers? What if I hadn't sought brutal feedback? What if I had just quit? If any of these had happened, I would not have a career as a writer. It all started with my willingness to change and adapt.

Adaptation to Expand My Work beyond Writing

My career as a writer coincided with the rise of the internet. When my first book was released, we did not have smartphones, social media, YouTube, OTT platforms, short video content like Instagram reels, influencers, WhatsApp, Zoom and online shopping. Today, all these things dominate our world. Even though I was successful as an author, I realized that just writing books would not be enough for me to stay relevant and connected to India's youth. I had to reach out to more people. This required me to adapt, yet again, to other new industries. Hence, I had to learn the ropes of how to break into Bollywood, which then adapted (no pun intended) my books into movies, making me a household name.

Over time, I also adapted to writing newspaper columns, working on TV shows, doing motivational talks on stage, being a part of OTT shows, managing a social media presence and becoming a YouTuber. All this has led me to be better known than many other writers in India. Literature experts may tell you that Chetan Bhagat is not the best writer. They are right. I'm not the best writer, but I'm a bestselling writer. And that is because I constantly evolve and adapt with time. In fact, this book is an attempt to adapt as well, as it is my first self-help/self-improvement book.

Learning to Adapt Better

For you to develop your ability to adapt, you need to honestly answer these questions first:

- Are you firm and fixed in your ways, thoughts, beliefs and ideologies?

- Do you need everything around you to be familiar and comfortable for you to work and function properly?

- Do you believe your point of view, your politics, your choice of career and friends is the correct one, and anyone who suggests otherwise is wrong?

- Do you find it hard to change, even though you know you must?

The more yeses you answer to the above, the more stuck-up you are. The truth is most of us are stuck-up. We have fixed ideas and opinions. We have habits and behaviours that are hard to change. Our brain literally fights change because it requires an uncomfortable rewiring and resetting of our already-set neural pathways. If you tried to clear an entrance exam three years in a row and it didn't work, you may need to rethink. Maybe this is not the exam for

> **Our brain literally fights change because it requires an uncomfortable rewiring and resetting of our already-set neural pathways.**

you, and you need a different career. If you are chasing
a relationship, but the other person doesn't care, you
need to adapt. Stop chasing and move on to something
else or someone else. If your customers are switching to
a competitor, you need to figure out why and adapt to a
better product or service.

Adapt or Fail: Examples from Business

Businesses must adapt over time as well. Only those who
can adapt, survive. Remember Blackberry and Nokia?
These brands once ruled the world of mobile phones.
Blackberry used to be huge during my banking days. It
had a simple black and white screen, along with a small
keypad with rows of tiny buttons. You could get emails
on this portable device, eliminating the need to keep
checking your desktop or laptop. Banking and corporate
executives were addicted to their Blackberrys. When I
quit my banking job to become a full-time writer, one
of the saddest things for me was returning the bank's
Blackberry. I had to buy another personal Blackberry on
the same day I left the bank to not let the emptiness get to
me! Today, Blackberry is nearly dead. This is ironical for a
tech company that was a worldwide rage less than fifteen
years ago. Nokia suffered a similar fate. Their presence
today is a tiny fraction of the omnipresent Nokia of the
early 2000s. Nokia and Blackberry missed adapting to

touchscreen phones and suffered for it. They did try to catch up later, but it was too late.

There are multiple examples of large corporations who lost the game. Always, it is a case of an inability to adapt. We may hate change, but we must change. For instance, we are currently witnessing the rise of electric vehicles. Only auto companies that can adapt their product lines to this change will thrive in the next decade. Similarly, artificial intelligence is seen as the future. Almost every tech company and many non-tech companies too will have to adapt to integrate artificial intelligence into their functioning and products if they want to survive.

> We may hate change, but we must change.

Have You Adapted?

Many of us study, get a degree in one subject, and hope to make a career in the same field. However, those days of one degree—one profession for life are gone. Let's say you are a doctor, a relatively stable field and career. You could remain a traditional doctor and probably hold a job. However, who are the richest doctors today? The ones who have understood business along with medicine. Doctors who can run a business can multiply their income manifold. They could open diagnostic centres, a scalable chain of clinics and online medical services.

Similarly, if you are in a job that doesn't pay well and the increments are poor, what should you do? You need to adapt and look for another, better role in the same company. Or, you need to change your job. To do any of this, you must adapt to learn networking, pitching yourself and figuring out opportunities. Another option to upgrade your career could be to start your own business. This requires a whole new degree of adaptation. You must enter unchartered territory, give up regular income and learn how to run a business.

Adaptation Outside the Realm of Your Career

Life will demand adaptation outside your career as well. As you grow older, your body will change. You will need to protect your health. In your twenties, you can get away with junk food and limited sleep. You cannot do the same in your forties. Those who adapt, continue to enjoy good health. Those who don't, start having health issues in their later years.

> Being a good boyfriend at eighteen isn't the same as being a good husband at thirty-eight.

Relationships demand adaptation too. Being a good boyfriend at eighteen isn't the same as being a good husband at thirty-eight. At eighteen, you probably just need to be fun and kind. At eighteen, Sandy on a motorbike may be enough for him to be considered cool. At thirty-eight, Sandy will need to be much more. He needs to be capable enough to take care of his family. Does Sandy have a good career? What about savings? Can Sandy buy a house? And your name is not Sandy, bro, its Sandeep. If Sandy never outgrew his motorbike adventures and did not adapt to have a successful career going, he will not be considered cool at thirty-eight.

Life is constantly evolving and changing, even though it may not seem that way on a day-to-day basis. Every day might seem the same as before. Hence you don't feel the need to change. But visualize your life ten years from now. What will be different? Where do you expect to be? What changes do you need to be making in yourself today to be where you want to be in the next ten years?

Mastering Adaptation

To sharpen your ability to adapt, start by embracing as much change as possible. I know people who will not even deviate from what they eat. I have friends who cannot do without the same Indian roti-subzi every day, even on a trip abroad. They almost make their rigidity an asset. 'I'm like this only, boss. I have to have my rotis with daal and dahi for every meal.' Well, you don't *have to*. You are simply used to it and too stubborn to change. That is why you are hunting for Indian restaurants in Paris. I know people who cringe at the idea of job transfers to another city in a different part of India. People from the north don't want to move to the south, and vice versa. 'I just love my own culture, people and language, you see,' is what they say in their defence. No, you are simply too stuck-up and rigid. Don't see a job transfer as a punishment. Embrace it and consider it an adventure. Company moving you to a different division? Great, go for it. Nobody knows you there? It's okay, adjust and learn how to make new friends. Kids' school will change? Well, they will adjust and learn to make new friends too.

> Whenever presented with options in life involving status quo or change, lean towards change. Over time, change won't scare you as much.

Whenever presented with options in life involving status quo or change, lean towards change. Over time, change won't scare you as much. Eventually, you will become as adaptive as a cockroach. Like a cockroach, you will also become chill about change and say, 'Things are changing? Great, bring it on. I will adjust!'

....

Key Takeaways

- You may not like change, but change is inevitable.
- In nature, or in real life, the most adaptive creature or person survives.
- Be chill about change. Don't be scared of it. Treat it like an adventure.

- The cockroach is the most adaptive creature on earth. Just like the cockroach survived for millions of years and adapted to every environment, adapt to changes around you.

- Anything can and will change—your career, relationships, status of your health, surroundings, etc. The key is to recognize it and adjust yourself to it.

....

'What should I change?' Viraj said.

'Meaning?' I said, twirling my bowl of tomato soup. I had ordered the lightest lunch possible—just a bowl of tomato soup with a tiny salad. The guilt of the two ice creams from two days ago had not left me.

'I will adapt like a cockroach. But what do I adapt to?' Viraj said.

'That's for you to decide. Ask yourself honestly and the answer will come.'

'The world is changing fast. If I remain a delivery boy, I won't get far.'

'It's never too late,' I said. 'There's nothing wrong in being a delivery boy. But if you think you can be more, go for it.'

'Yes, I must adapt and get a new career. Maybe study. Get another degree. A useful one,' Viraj said and stood up to leave.

'Good, I see you are thinking.'

'Yes, I will think about my life. I will ask myself, "What would a cockroach do?"'

'New role model?'

'Sort of. What do we talk about tomorrow?'

'Connections. That's Rule Nine. Connecting with people.'

RULE #9

LEARN TO CONNECT WITH PEOPLE

'Networking is not about who you know, it's about who knows you.'

—UNKNOWN

Networking is key to success in life, learn it.

One Can of Chole

A few years into my banking job at Goldman Sachs, I was stuck with a terrible boss. I will call him Toxic T. He made my life a living hell. Toxic T criticized me, took good assignments away from me, denied me a promotion twice and generally made my life unpleasant at work. I wanted to quit. Unfortunately, this was in the early 2000s. The dotcom bubble had burst. There were no openings in finance. I wouldn't find another job for months.

Around that time, on a weekend, I was roaming around a shopping mall called Pacific Place in Hong

Kong. There, I ran into my first boss from my first job in Hong Kong, which had been at a firm called Peregrine. His name was Damien Wood, a friendly Australian guy in his thirties. He now worked at Credit Suisse and headed Credit Research. In Peregrine, I had worked under him, writing Credit Research reports. We chatted for a few minutes at the mall, exchanging polite conversation. We almost waved each other goodbye, but on an impulse, I asked him, 'Damien, do you like home-cooked Indian food?'

'I love Indian food,' he replied.

'Why don't you come home for dinner this weekend?' I said. 'I can make some Indian-style chickpeas.'

'I love chickpeas. I love Indian food in general. It's so exotic. Great, see you.'

And just like that, I invited him home. I had chosen chickpeas (chole or chana) for a reason. They are easy to make. In Hong Kong, you can easily get cans of boiled chickpea in the supermarket. You also get pureed tomato in cans. Take these two ingredients, stir-fry them with a few Indian spices and you have chana masala. I also made some boiled rice, and my exotic Indian dinner was ready.

Damien came with his wife. My wife and I had a fun dinner with them. This was the first time Damien and I had met outside of work. For dessert, I served them fresh Alphonso mangoes, bought from the Indian store. Towards the end of dinner, I mentioned to Damien in passing, 'I'm not particularly happy at Goldman Sachs.'

'Oh, really?' Damien said, eating a slice of the Alphonso. 'Why? By the way, these mangoes are delicious.'

'I have this difficult boss. Plus, I miss writing research content like I did for you at Peregrine. And yes, this is considered the best variety of mangoes in the world.'

The dinner ended soon after. Damien and his wife thanked us and left.

Two months later, Damien called me. 'Would you consider moving to Credit Suisse?'

I said an immediate yes. I left Goldman Sachs, and was rid of Toxic T for life. (Toxic T read about my becoming famous years later when he saw my name in *Time* magazine's 100 Most Influential People list, but that's a story for another time.) I moved to Credit Suisse. My reports there got me noticed. From there I moved on to Deutsche Bank, where I worked in their lucrative distressed debt group. That job in Deutsche Bank helped me make and save good money in my final years in banking. Those savings finally allowed me to quit my banking job and become a full-time writer.

That's it. All this happened because I bumped into Damien Wood at the mall and invited him home. One can of chole changed my entire life.

Connecting with people matters a lot. If I had not connected with Damien, not invited him home, my life would be totally different today.

Half Girlfriend

Another example of the power of connections comes from much later in my life. I often go to a gym near my house in Bandra, Mumbai. A few years ago, sometime in 2014, I was on the elliptical trainer. An older gentleman was walking on a treadmill next to me. With a thin and wiry frame, he was probably in his early sixties. We exchanged smiles. After that day, we greeted each other in the gym every time we met. One day, we introduced ourselves to each other. He was Mukesh Bhatt, a Bollywood producer. I told him about my upcoming book, a love story titled *Half Girlfriend*. He in turn introduced me to his nephew, Mohit Suri, a film director specializing in love stories. I met Mohit, one thing led to another, and we ended up co-producing *Half Girlfriend*. The movie released in 2017. Of course, all this became possible only because I was well known at that point. However, the movie *Half Girlfriend* would never have happened, and I would never have become co-producer of a movie if I hadn't smiled and greeted the older gentleman at the gym.

The Power of Connections

Business invariably happens because of connections. You must learn how to connect with other human beings in such a way that you become part of a greater network that will eventually bring you benefits. A big advantage of being in a higher societal class is that you get to make connections with other people who are higher up in the class order. A Class III (Worker/Slave/Drone) is less likely to have connections with Class IIs or Class Is. However, top doctors often know top lawyers who know top accountants.

> You must learn how to connect with other human beings in such a way that you become part of a greater network that will eventually bring you benefits.

You often see pictures of top industrialists, actors and politicians hanging out together. This is the crème de la crème of Indian society, perhaps the top 0.01 per cent of the high-status people in the country. Even they like to network. You, who still have a long way to go in life, must keep polishing your networking skills.

What Is a Network?

A network is simply several interconnected points. When it comes to human networks, each person is a point. Your relationship with others is the interconnection. All of us are connected to people around us, such as close family and friends. However, networking goes much further. Networking isn't about close friends or partying together. Networking involves establishing a relationship with a wide variety and a large number of people. The relationship should be such that if you choose to reach out to them at some point in life, they will respond to you. They may or may not be your friends. But they do know you, respect you and care enough to reciprocate communication. If it makes sense for them, they will also help you.

Damien Wood wasn't my close friend. However, we had spent a few months working together and he was my first boss when I arrived in Hong Kong, straight out of campus. Damien and I maintained a decent enough relationship so when we ran into each other years later at the mall we could chat for a few minutes. This is what I meant by reciprocating each other's communication. The next step was my asking him over for dinner. At that point I didn't really have an agenda. It was just a way for me to keep the connection alive. Damien probably evaluated the dinner invite and felt it would be fun as he liked Indian food and wanted to connect with me as well. It made sense to him to accept my invitation. At dinner, I told him about being unhappy at Goldman Sachs. I didn't ask Damien for a job. However, luckily, a few months later when he had an opportunity at his firm, it made sense to him to reach out to me. He would fulfil his hiring need and I would get a new job. My networking with him paid off well. It eventually changed my life. However, there was always the possibility that nothing would result

> ❦ Not every connection will pay off. That's why you need a lot of them. ⬧

from that dinner or my connection with him. That's fine. Not every connection will pay off. That's why you need a lot of them. Another probable scenario—Damien could have referred me to someone else in his network, who could then have helped me find a new job. In that case, my network would have connected to his network. This is what happened when Mukesh Bhatt, the person I networked with at the gym, connected me to Mohit Suri, another person in his network.

Networking for Success

People who are driven and successful not only work a lot, but also network a lot. They understand that the world is ultimately run by people. People are driven by their own needs. Sometimes there is a win-win when there is a match between your need and their need. Someone needs to hire a person. You need a job. Someone is looking for a script. You have a script to offer. Boom! People connect and everyone gains. However, all this happens only if you first cultivate a vast network of your own. They say your network is your net worth. It is true. Your network is just as valuable as the wealth you possess, if not more.

> Your network is just as valuable as the wealth you possess, if not more.

How to Improve Your Network

Step 1: Get in Front of More People

Networking is about people. The first step is to ensure you interact with a lot of people. Your school, college and office are obvious places to start. How many people do you know there? Are these people your immediate classmates or colleagues? Why not increase the number of people you mingle with? Take part in activities, help organize things, initiate conversation with people in the cafeteria. All of these count. Outside of work, there are opportunities in places like the gym, activity classes, volunteer organizations, your apartment complex, and basically any place where you can connect with other people. Virtual networking helps too. LinkedIn, Facebook groups, and other online communities can help you get started with a virtual network, which hopefully you can convert to real life one day.

Step 2: Learn to Talk to People

Merely being connected with people or joining organizations is not enough. You should leave some kind of impact on others for them to remember you. Learn to engage people in a conversation with you. Ensure they enjoy talking to you and remember you after the interaction is over.

It's easier to do this if you already belong to Class I or Class II, or have something to offer the other person. If a top actress or sportsman enters the room, they don't have to make massive effort and be amazing conversationalists to get everyone's attention. Everyone is just happy to be around them. You, who still

> Learn to engage people in a conversation with you. Ensure they enjoy talking to you and remember you after the interaction is over.

have some way to go in life, must learn to charm people. At a minimum, you should be able to engage any person in a conversation for five minutes that they enjoy and feel good about later.

How does one do that? I could give you some quick hacks or a checklist of conversation topics or questions to ask people. However, that would be formulaic and will not work. What works is authenticity. You must genuinely, truly be interested in people. Think of each person as the star of a movie called their life. Now imagine you have come to watch this movie, and it is up to you to get the best scenes out of them.

People like to talk about themselves and what they feel passionately about. Ask open-ended questions about them or their work. Say you meet someone at your building society gathering who is a

> What works is authenticity. You must genuinely, truly be interested in people.

doctor. You can ask them where they work, which may be a start. However, that isn't an open-ended question. They will just answer Apollo Hospital or something, and that's it. However, if you ask them an open-ended question such as, 'What is the best and the worst part about being a doctor?' they have to give a longer, thought-through response. Since you have asked about something related to them, they are likely to be more interested in answering it. Once they respond, continue to make genuine, curious queries. For instance, 'What was the most interesting case you have ever worked on?' Or, if they say, 'The best part about being a doctor is you can save lives,' you can follow up with, 'Do you remember the first time you saved someone's life? What was that like?'

There isn't any prescribed method for talking to people. It is an art and skill developed with practise. All this, however, is not taught or emphasized in our schools and colleges. There are some frameworks on how to continue a meaningful conversation. One of them is FORD, which stands for Family, Occupation, Recreation and Dreams. Ask people about any of these topics and you will mostly be okay.

Talking to People: Things to Watch Out For

Avoid controversial topics such as politics or religion, especially in the initial stages of getting to know a person. A good way to show interest in people is to ask about their feelings, especially how they feel about the work they do. If the person in front of you is senior to you in age, status or education, you can also seek some light advice.

However, don't expect them to be your career counsellor, mentor or therapist. You don't want to give them work to do. When you ask for their advice, it is in effect a form of praise to convey that you look up to them. Let us say you meet the owner of a successful business. You can ask, 'I'm thinking of quitting my job and starting

> Avoid controversial topics such as politics or religion, especially in the initial stages of getting to know a person. A good way to show interest in people is to ask about their feelings, especially how they feel about the work they do.

my own business. As a successful businessperson, what are the top two pieces of advice you would give me?' Simple, that's it. They can give whatever answer they want. You thank them for it. Notice the genuine 'successful businessperson' compliment in the question.

Do not ask them, 'Can you help me make my business plan?', or worse, 'Can you give me some money to start a business?' You have nothing to offer and no leverage yet. The best you can do is have an interesting conversation with them. After the interaction, exchange numbers. Stay in touch. Maybe send them an interesting article related to their work on WhatsApp once every two months. Don't spam them, don't forward junk and definitely don't send them 'good morning' texts every day.

Eventually, it is about calibration. Engage with them at a level where they feel good about hearing from you, but not overwhelmed. Occasionally, you can ask for a personal meeting, perhaps to see their clinic, shop or factory. Have more conversations. Repeat this with all the people you meet, particularly those who are doing well in life and those whom you want to be like. In a few years, if not months, you will have created a good network of people.

Finally, before you approach anyone in your network, always think of why you are approaching them. Are you doing it just to keep the network alive? That's fine. Or do you want something? If you want something, what do you have to offer? Do not ask for something with nothing to offer in return.

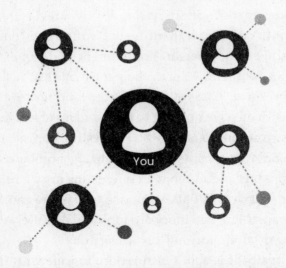

NETWORKING: THE VARIOUS NODES ARE THE PEOPLE IN YOUR LIFE. THE LINES ARE THE RELATIONSHIPS.

Networking Up versus Networking Down

For your own success, you may always want to network up, or build a network with people higher in status than you. However, this isn't always how real life works. True, networking is not only about your career gains. Career gains are a by-product of being a well-networked person, which itself comes from being a great people person.

Don't think too much about whether you are networking up or down. Think about developing your people skills. How can I make an impact on people when I meet them? How do I keep in touch without coming across as too clingy or bothersome? Think 'How can I help this person?' not 'How can this person help me?' Eventually, you'll be able to build a tight and trusted network that will pay off over time.

> ❝ Don't think too much about whether you are networking up or down. Think about developing your people skills. ❞

Of course, don't only network down either. Networking up is a good thing. You have to put in extra effort to network with people who are above you in status. When you start really low, you are unlikely to get access to people who have an ultra-high status. Make the most of what you have. Keep working on yourself, do what it takes to move ahead in your career in order to improve your status. You will eventually meet people who have higher status. Value your network. And never forget, your network is your net worth.

....

Key Takeaways

- Your network is your net worth.

- Networking requires maintaining healthy connections with a wide variety and number of people. The relationship should be such that if you choose to reach out to them at some point in life, they will respond to you.

- Not every connection in your network will pay off. But some will. And that's why you must focus on having a wide network of connections.

- To have a wide network you have to be around people and be genuinely interested in them.

- Interact with people from all classes, the ones above you and the ones below you too. Any connection may lead to anything at any time.

....

Viraj had brought me Chinese food today. It came from a restaurant called China House. The noodles tasted delicious, as did the dumplings that came along with it.

'It is like these noodles,' I said. 'Your network is these intermingled relationships with other people, helping you go through life.'

'Sorry, Chetan sir. I'm sorry, but this rule is not for me,' Viraj said.

'Why?' I looked at him, surprised.

'I'm just a delivery boy. How and whom will I network with? I can never network up.'

'I don't understand.'

'What do you expect? I deliver food in Bandra to a businessman, and start chatting with him? He won't even speak to me. In most cases, the security guard will collect the packet. Even if I go to deliver it, the most I will get is a little tip, not a chance at conversation.'

'That's probably true, yes.'

'The gap is too big. They see delivery people as ... Actually, they don't even see us. We are just machines who get them their sandwiches and biryani.'

'What about the restaurants, though?'

'Restaurants?'

'You spend time outside restaurants, right?'

'A lot. Waiting for them to finish preparing the food.'

'How many times have you spoken to the manager there?'

'What do you mean?'

'*You don't only go to fancy restaurants, right? Most of the restaurants people order from are simpler, cheaper ones.*'

'*True.*'

'*Have you ever spoken to the manager of a small restaurant? Asked them more about themselves or their job?*'

'*Me? How can I?*'

'*Why not?*'

'*I'm only a delivery partner. Plus, at peak times managers are busy.*'

'*What about when it's not peak time? Have you even tried?*'

Viraj paused to think. He shook his head.

'*Why not?*'

Viraj did not answer. I continued. 'What about the job recruitment agency that helped you get this job? Did you ever chat and network with the staff there?'

Viraj looked at me. It was his turn to be surprised. He shook his head. I spoke again.

'*You never thought of that, Viraj, did you? Even though the people in the agency know of all the jobs in the market. They aren't even much higher in status than you. They are accessible.*'

Viraj nodded.

'Did you join any puja organizing society in your area? Like for Ganpati or Durga Puja? Any other place you can help? Like an NGO?'

'All this has never even crossed my mind.'

'It should. Too bad we never teach this to students. How to network.'

'Let me go to the recruitment agency today.'

'Just like that?'

'I know a bakery in Bandra. They give away unsold stock at night. I will take some bakery items for the agency staff.'

'Excellent. See, the bakery is in your network. They give you the items for free. The cookies and cakes you take to the agency are the value you offer to the agency staff.'

'And the information they will give me about the new jobs is the value I can get from them.'

'Exactly. Maybe they will not give you that information immediately. But, some day, they might. For now, just strengthen the network.'

'Yes. Thank you.'

'Welcome. See you tomorrow, for Rule Ten.'

RULE #10

IT'S MY FAULT

'Extreme ownership. Leaders must own everything in their world. There is no one else to blame.'

—JOCKO WILLINK

Taking accountability for your actions is the first step to make things better.

The Fat Boy Who Learnt Zodiac Signs

I was a fat child. ('Fat' may not be the most politically correct term these days, but I prefer using it to describe my past self.) I was a fat grown-up as well, for most of my life. The first time I was made fun of for being overweight was in school. I had a paunch. Some of my classmates liked to poke at the soft layer of fat on my stomach. They found it hilarious. They would laugh at me. To avoid the humiliation, I would laugh along with them. Being fat meant I wasn't good at sports, and hence wasn't selected for any of the school sports teams.

I reached senior classes. Boys and girls had started having crushes on each other. I realized being fat also meant girls in my class didn't look at me as much. I had, for the most part, accepted my fate. There were the handsome and fit guys, and I wasn't one of them. 'It's okay, everyone in life can't be handsome,' I used to tell myself. Or, I would have a mental dialogue like, 'They might be handsome and have biceps, but I am good at Maths. I scored 90 per cent, they scored 70 per cent.' Somehow, to me, my knowledge of calculus compensated for my physical appearance. I tried various ways to talk to girls. I would learn jokes to make them laugh. Girls like a good sense of humour, don't they?

I prepared topics girls around me liked to talk about, such as English music and zodiac signs. I read *Linda Goodman's Sun Signs*. If the girl was a Virgo, I would mug up the traits of a Virgo to speak to her.

'Are you quite emotional, and do more for your friends than they do for you?' I would say to the Virgo girl.

'Oh yes, how true! How do you know?' she'd say. (Who would deny something like that anyway.)

'It's a Virgo thing. You are a Virgo, right? You also value love more than money … blah blah blah,' I would add, hoping to continue the conversation.

To a certain extent, I did succeed in talking to girls using this method. 'So what if I am fat and have a paunch? I know how to talk to girls,' I told myself.

Yes, girls did talk to me. However, that's where it ended. They would never, ever find me attractive, look at me in a romantic way or date me. That was reserved for the captain of the basketball team. I would crush on a girl. We would discuss sun signs all day. I would propose to her. She would reject me. This happened many times. Often, they rebuffed me in the nicest, cutest way. Here are some examples.

'Aww, how sweet, you like me. But I don't see you *that* way.'

'Well, I like you too, but only *as a friend*. Let's not spoil what we have.'

'I like you. But in a *teddy bear, buddy* kind of way.'

'You are so cute and roly-poly. It's funny to imagine you as a boyfriend.'

You see the pattern? They were letting me down easy. It still hurt. Friend-zoning hurts, and the only thing that hurts more is another category Indian girls have invented to ward off guys they are not attracted to—the Rakhi brother.

Anyway, I am sure all this has happened to many guys. Men face rejection from women all the time. It's not really the women's fault. They are not part of an evil admissions committee looking to reject guys or hurt them. Women get approached by a lot of men and they can't date them all. Nor can they date a guy if they do not feel attracted to him. At that time, though, I didn't see things in this holistic way. I only felt rejected and hurt, and took it very personally. I thought the girl rejecting my proposal was sadistic and enjoyed hurting me.

'Why did she lead me on, talking to me for hours about Virgos and Scorpios when she wasn't interested? Why did she speak to me on the phone every day?' I would think, crying myself to sleep.

At other times, I would be angry. 'She's so dumb. She can see that she enjoys talking to me. I make her laugh. Yet she's going around with that cricket captain. How stupid can she be?' Hence, to me, girls were either evil or stupid. I was simply a good boy trying to express my feelings for a girl. I felt the girls gave me this pain. In other words, I said, 'It's their fault.' *They* were responsible for my heartbreak. *They* were at fault. Not me.

We deflect our real issues all the time, exactly like I did. In our minds, we create a narrative that comforts us in that moment but harms us in the long term. It is the same infamous template of the victimhood narrative.

'If only others behaved better, my life would be better.'

Once this narrative sets in, variations of it sit in our heads. Here are some examples, many from my own life.

- 'My childhood sucked, that's why I can't do well at anything in life.'
- 'I don't have supportive parents, that's why I am not achieving what I want to.'

- 'My parents are too pushy, and that's why I'm incapable of doing anything now.'

- 'We are Punjabis, we love food too much. That's why I am fat.'

- 'I didn't get enough love as a child. That's why I overeat and have become fat.'

- 'The entire education system sucks. That's why I can't get admission in a good place.'

- 'My bones are too heavy. It's genetics. That's why I am overweight.'

- 'My parents aren't rich or well-connected. That's why I can't get ahead in life.'

- 'My friends distract me. That's why I can't study.'

- 'There's just too much competition these days. I just won't succeed.'

- 'The government has not created enough jobs. That's why I can't get a good job.'

This list of reasons to deflect blame on others can be endless. We come up with perfect-sounding explanations (or excuses, rather) for the current state of our body, income, status and quality of life. We all have our reasons to justify why we are where we are in life. Perhaps this is a coping mechanism for us humans. If we continue to feel inadequate and blame ourselves for all our shortcomings, we will feel miserable. Hence, the brain, like a generative AI model, creates a list like the one above where the essence of each line is the same.

'If only others behaved better, my life would be better.'

Cool, that's it then. Let's accept how things are. Let's stop trying to improve. All your problems and shortcomings are because of other people. You can't do anything about that. Close this book, toss it away and keep living a mediocre life. Whenever that little voice in your head asks you to do better, pull out a reason or excuse from your master excuse list and do nothing.

The result of this will be that nothing will change, you will never improve and eventually you will die having lived a mediocre life. Fine, welcome to how 99 per cent of humanity lives.

Or, you can do things differently. You can break the narrative of blaming others. Even if your reasons or excuses are genuine, they still don't help. You can't control other people. Even if we agree it really is their fault, your problem won't get fixed until those people change themselves. You can't make them do that. You can only do one thing—change yourself. Even that is extremely difficult. Over the years, we become so pig-headed and our beliefs so rigid that it becomes a challenge to rewrite the code in our neural circuits. However, it is still possible to change. Our brains have neuroplasticity, and we can learn to think better, be better, and live better lives. The first step in this process is clearing out the garbage justifications list in your head and replacing it with another simple new belief and narrative:

'*It's my fault.*'

Taking Extreme Accountability

If something is not working in your life, your default response should be to take responsibility by saying, 'It's my fault.' Your friend makes more money than you? You think it is because he got lucky and got that MNC job. No. It's your fault. You are responsible for not trying harder. You should have put ten times more effort while searching for a job.

> If something is not working in your life, your default response should be to take responsibility by saying, "It's my fault."

Girls kept friend-zoning me and called me a teddy bear? It's not because they were evil or ignorant. It was *my* fault. I was fat and unattractive. Instead of cramming details of zodiac signs, I should have gone for a run or exercised every day.

Sadly, I did not take accountability for my being overweight at that time. I grew from a fat kid into a fat adult. I made excuses and did not put in real effort to change anything. I remained fat. Being overweight becomes a bigger issue as you get older. There's overwhelming scientific evidence to show that excess weight increases the risk of heart disease, diabetes, high blood pressure and other ailments. These are some of the leading causes of death in humans. Excess weight can literally kill you. But I kept living the way I did.

Fixing Myself

I finally realized in my forties that I was putting my health in danger. The time I got to think during the Covid lockdowns helped me realize I was doing it all wrong. And only I could fix it. Things changed for me when I said enough is enough to the nonsense beliefs in my own head. There's nothing Punjabi-specific about eating unhealthy food. No matter who you are—Punjabi, Tamilian, Bengali, Mexican or Chinese—you can make healthier choices. I cut out the obvious junk from my diet—processed foods and anything too oily or too sweet. I did intermittent fasting. I also realized exercise is for everyone, not just 'sporty' people. God didn't make humans sporty or non-sporty. Even if we've never played a sport or don't know what to do in a gym, we can all start with a little run. I became a runner, and started with a few kilometres every day.

Was it hard to change my diet and go for a daily run? Yes, incredibly so. However, at least I began doing something about a problem I had faced all my life—being fat.

Once I took accountability, I had something specific to do to change the situation, like cut down on unhealthy food and exercise more. This only happened because I said, *It's my fault*.

If you have an EJL, or an Excuses and Justifications List, in your head, rip it out for good. Many motivational experts encourage this concept of extreme accountability. Every single aspect of your life, from the shirt you are wearing to the career you have, is your responsibility. Never succumb to the temptation of getting comfortable with your EJL. The EJL will make you feel better for a while. However, it will ultimately leave your problem unsolved, and your life will remain a mediocre mess.

> ❝ If you have an EJL, or an Excuses and Justifications List, in your head, rip it out for good. ❞

> ❝ Never succumb to the temptation of getting comfortable with your EJL. The EJL will make you feel better for a while. However, it will ultimately leave your problem unsolved, and your life will remain a mediocre mess. ❞

You had terrible parents? That is indeed sad. But did you let that define every aspect of your life? Did you stop working hard because of it? Or did you double your efforts to get out of that situation? It's your responsibility. I could have used whatever happened in my childhood as an excuse to start smoking, maybe move on to other drugs. Horrible childhood, you see? How am I expected to study physics? Well, no. I told myself I'd better study physics. What was happening wasn't my fault, but if I ignored my studies, it would be my fault.

Your spouse is not understanding or supportive of your goals? Well, it's still your fault. You are an emotional idiot if you need your spouse's validation and support to chase your goals. If they really are your goals, chase away at them with as much determination as you can, with or without support.

Do you lack focus and concentration? It's because of the many distractions on your phone. You are addicted to cheap dopamine. Only you can get out of it.

> This book can guide you on the right path to make your life a success. However, only *you* can make it happen.

Remember, nobody is coming to save you in this world. Nobody cares. Perhaps your parents do, but only up to a point. Remain a loser long enough and even your parents will give up. This book can guide you on the right path to make your life a success. However, only *you* can make it happen. The reason you don't have a six-pack (neither do I), or enough money, or a great romantic partner is all your fault.

But once you take extreme accountability and acknowledge it

> Once you take responsibility, you can replace everything you don't have with a "yet" at the end. "I don't have six-pack" becomes "I don't have a six-pack, yet".

is your fault, a plan will emerge. You can then act on this plan, fix your problem and get yourself to a better place. Once you take responsibility, you can replace everything you don't have with a 'yet' at the end. 'I don't have six-pack' becomes 'I don't have a six-pack, yet'. You don't have enough money, yet. You don't have a great girlfriend or boyfriend, yet. But you can fix it. One little step at a time. (And yes, I am going to keep working towards that six-pack!)

The Brutal Truth Augmented-Reality Mirror

One of my favourite motivators is ex-US Navy Seal and ultra-marathoner David Goggins. He has wonderful videos and books, and I highly recommend them. He talks about the concept of the 'accountability mirror' in his book *Can't Hurt Me*. As a hat tip to him, I would like to talk about my own modified BTAR Mirror, or Brutal Truth Augmented-Reality Mirror.

Imagine a beautiful mirror. Now stand in front of it. It shows you your entire body. You can see the scars, pimples, dirt and the areas of your body where you are fat. Now imagine the same mirror with enhanced Brutal Truth Augmented-Reality features. Whenever you stand in front of this mirror, it not only shows you your physical body in detail, but also tells you about your life. It tells you what is good, but more importantly, it tells you what sucks.

Imagine this mirror with someone called Manish standing in front of it. Manish can see his face and body. On a display alongside, he can also see some statements.

- 'Manish is fat. He needs to lose 10 kilograms to look his best, feel his best and prevent diseases.'

- 'Manish is anxious about his career. He feels he could be laid off. However, he has made no backup plans.'

- 'Manish is ignoring his parents, even though he knows that relationship is important.'

- 'Manish has not invested his money properly. He doesn't even have a clear idea of where and how his money is kept.'

- 'Manish has only gone to the gym twice in the last month. His membership is going waste.'

Now replace Manish with your name and read the above statements again.

Will it be scary for you to stand in front of such a mirror? Possibly. However, will it be beneficial? Absolutely. It is always better to be aware of the areas of your life that need work. If you don't know what you need to fix, how will you fix it?

> It is always better to be aware of the areas of your life that need work. If you don't know what you need to fix, how will you fix it?

While the technology for such a mirror does not exist yet, we can all create a brutal-truth mirror for ourselves. We don't even need to stand in front of an actual mirror for this. We simply need to understand the reality of our lives. We need to list out the things that are not in order. It's a simple exercise. Yet we don't do it. We don't want to face our problems and take responsibility.

What do we do instead? We throw dust on our brutal-truth mirror and deliberately make it hazy so we can't see clearly. When we have problems in life, we mask them with alcohol, smoking, binging on video content, TV, video games and social media. We do this to pass our time, numb our pain and take our attention away from our problems. We throw a shiny layer of cheap dopamine on our brutal-truth mirror, to avoid the pain of clear reality. Ultimately, the problems fester and become bigger. The 10 kilograms overweight becomes 20 kilograms overweight, which later causes a heart attack. Zero career focus at twenty-five leads to becoming broke at forty-five, which then turns into poverty in old age.

> Your purpose in life is taking responsibility for yourself, fixing your issues and becoming the best person you can possibly be.

Wipe the dust off your brutal-truth mirror. Place it in extra-bright sunlight, and then ask it to tell you everything. List out everything that sucks in your life. Then say, 'Yes, it's all true, and it's all my fault.' Chart out a plan to fix each problem. Go on a journey to repair your life and make yourself a better person. You wanted a purpose in life? There, you have it. Your purpose in life is taking responsibility for yourself, fixing your issues and becoming the best person you can possibly be.

···

Key Takeaways

■ If you keep blaming others and circumstances, you will continue to live a mediocre, miserable life.

■ Junk your Excuses and Justifications List, your EJL, and replace it with extreme accountability—you are the problem but you are also the solution.

■ Take reality by the horns—learn to solve your issues instead of brushing them under the carpet.

■ When you acknowledge that whatever is not right is your fault, you will be able to think of a plan you can act upon to change things.

···

'It's all my fault,' Viraj said, nodding to himself. 'Yes, it is my fault.'

'What is your fault?' I said.

'My life and all my problems. I have made it what it is. I could have done better.'

I opened my lunch box. I had ordered a bowl of rajma-rice from a newly opened cloud kitchen. It came in a nice Instagramable circular bowl, divided in two halves with the rajma curry in one section and the steamed rice in the other.

Viraj insisted I eat while I spoke to him. I offered to share. He declined. He was counting calories.

'This time no confusion, no counter argument about the "it's your fault" rule?' I said.

'Actually, I do have counter arguments,' Viraj said.

'Ah, see. I knew it. I feel worried if you get so easily convinced. Okay, go ahead. Make your counter arguments.'

'You say it's all your fault,' Viraj started. 'But what if someone gets cancer? Or a bus hits them? Or someone's parent dies when they are young. Everything is not always your own fault.'

'You are right. That can be the case sometimes,' I said.

Viraj paused to think as I blew air over the spoonful of hot rajma–rice. He spoke again.

'No, I am not right. I am citing exceptions but missing the point. Yes, some people can be hit by huge, unexpected *misfortune. But I don't have cancer. I haven't been run over by a bus. I simply had to work harder and be more focused. I didn't, so yes, it's my fault.'*

'You have come a long way, Viraj. From protesting about every rule to resolving doubts yourself.'

'They aren't doubts. They are another form of excuses. When we have good advice, we know it. If we still purposefully look for some tiny exception as evidence to prove it wrong, it's another form of denial and making excuses. I don't want to do that anymore.'

'That's well put, Viraj. Finally, it comes down to the beliefs that serve us. It's just better to believe that the fault lies within you, because then the power to fix things also lies with you. If you say, "But in this exceptional case" or "But it really was not completely that person's fault"—'

Viraj interrupted me to complete my sentence.

'It won't help. If I keep on saying, "Arpita hurt me," how does it benefit me? Arpita didn't hurt me. She didn't do or ask me to do anything. I was a fool. I decided to chase her instead of chasing my goals. I am an idiot. She only did what was best for her. And I could not give her that. I ignored my life. Yes, loud and clear, it's my fault.'

Viraj stood up to leave.

'What's the plan going forward?' I said.

'I am working on a plan. There's still one last rule left though, right?'

'Yes, just one. A simple, practical but often ignored one.'

'What is it?'

'Tomorrow,' I smiled.

RULE #11

EARN, SAVE AND INVEST

'The best time to plant a tree was twenty years ago. The second-best time is now.'

—CHINESE PROVERB

You cannot become rich just by earning a salary in a job. You have to learn to save and invest that money.

My Friend D

I have a friend. Let's call him Dinesh (name changed) or D. Dinesh and I have been friends from college. Our relationship goes back decades. We are both close to fifty now. D lost his finance job during the industrywide layoffs one year ago. He has not found another job yet. This is making D anxious. Recently, I met him in a bar.

'The market is bad. Nobody is hiring in my area. Plus, at my age, it's doubly hard to get a job,' D complained, gulping his whisky as if it were Coke.

'It's okay, D. You worked for decades. You don't have to rush to get back. Take a break. Focus on other aspects of your life,' I said.

D took out a pack of cigarettes.

'Do you mind if I smoke?' he said.

'No. But you should quit. Cigarettes have many negative health effects and—'

'Fine, Mister Motivational Speaker,' D cut me short. 'Give me a break. I am unemployed. Nobody wants me. I need something in my life to perk me up.'

'This won't help. I mean, it will, temporarily. But eventually it will make it worse.'

D nodded in agreement but lit a cigarette anyway. I decided to spare him the lecture on dopamine circuits and how cigarettes will mess them up.

'I am okay with temporary relief,' D said. 'You have no idea what I am going through.'

'Why, D? Haven't you worked for decades? I'm sure you have savings. I say quit this daily corporate drudgery forever. Live a free life. Try something new.'

D shook his head. 'I don't have the luxury of that choice like you, Mister Writer. I must work like a donkey. Do the drudgery.'

'Why?'

'There's an EMI on the new house. Kids' school is expensive. Their college will be even more so. Car loan, household staff, bills, running the house. It's all cash flowing out. Nothing is coming in.'

'What about savings? Investments? Assets?' I said.

'What savings? There isn't much. I need to work, bhai. We are not lucky like you.'

Luxury of choice. Lucky. That is how D described me. He wasn't wrong. I did choose not to work in a corporate. I hadn't for the last fifteen years, and I wasn't planning to either. I still remember drafting my farewell email at Deutsche Bank, my last employer. I felt nervous and scared before I pressed send, but I did it.

As D would say, I could quit banking because I was 'lucky' enough to be a bestselling writer. I do accept some element of luck in my becoming a writer. I have worked hard, but so do many other writers who never reach the level of recognition I have.

Quitting Banking for Writing

However, D was getting it somewhat wrong too. He thought I could quit my job because I had a writing career that paid well. But that wasn't the case when I quit my banking job. When I left investment banking, writing didn't pay me well. At that time, my writing income was less than 5 per cent of what I made in banking. That meant a 95 per cent drop in my income. Very few people quit their jobs for a 95 per cent drop, but I did. Even that 5 per cent of writing income wasn't safe. I had some popularity then, but what if my readers had moved on to another upcoming writer? What if they had forgotten about Chetan Bhagat? My writing income, however little, would have fallen to zero.

I would love to say I still took the risk and quit my job because I am super brave. I just jumped off a building towards my passion, believing I could fly and soar—and look, a writer was born! It makes for a great story. However, it isn't entirely true. I did jump to fly off, but I also ensured I had a safety net below so I didn't crash and die. That safety net was my financial planning. The safety net was made of my savings and investments, which I had been stocking away for years. Hence, it isn't just my writing but also my financial planning that helped me quit my regular job at thirty-five.

However, D couldn't do it even at fifty. To see how this happened, let's go back in time.

D and I: First Job

D and I started work at the same time, in similar-paying jobs abroad. Both of us lived in Hong Kong, an expensive city. If one wasn't careful, it was easy to spend the entire salary of an entry-level financial analyst by the end of the month. I was a saver; D was not. D and some other analysts at my level rented homes in fancier expat buildings close to work. I chose to live in a less posh, more local, Chinese area further away. I paid USD 1,500 a month as rent; others paid USD 3,000. The saving I made on rent versus the others was USD 1,500 a month, or USD 18,000 per year. Our salaries including bonuses were around USD 60,000 a year. Hence, I saved 30 per cent of my salary by downgrading my residence alone.

I saved in other areas too. I ate at home rather than eating out. I spent less on leisure trips. I took public transport instead of taxis. Despite crunching it on many fronts, I managed to have fun. Hong Kong is cool no matter where you live. Some of my friends found me weird, even if they didn't say it. However, after five years, I had substantial savings, and the others did not. They did get to live in nicer homes at the time. But, later, I believe I got to live a nicer life without the need to be a corporate slave.

D—The Man Who Knew How to Live

I always saved. D never did. In the early 2000s, we did not have phrases like YOLO (You Only Live Once). However, D embodied YOLO before the term became mainstream. He had a lovely apartment with a stunning view of the Hong Kong harbour. He lived in a posh area called Upper Mid-levels, up on a hill. Everyone who visited his house was instantly impressed. He had done up his house well, with expensive furniture and art. He had an elaborate bar, with crystal decanters and aged whiskies from around the world. People who came to D's house told him he had 'great taste' and that 'he knew how to live life'. As our salaries improved in banking, so did D's lifestyle. He moved to a bigger and more beautiful house. His family grew. He had kids and so he moved to an even larger place. He also bought a new luxury car and took a country club membership. His savings remained meagre.

However, as they say—YOLO! You only live once! The only problem is that living once also means living and planning for your entire life, and not just that moment.

Investing

Not only did I save, I also learnt to invest. I had no idea about investing in stock markets. Then, months into my first job, I opened a brokerage account with the help of an office colleague. I bought shares worth USD 5,000, an amount which constituted my entire savings at that point. As a novice, I bought shares of the company I worked for, Peregrine, because I didn't know any other company in Hong Kong. It was a rookie mistake, as I did not diversify from where I worked, and I paid for it. Peregrine went bankrupt and shut down in six months due to the Asian financial crisis of 1997. I lost my job *and* my Peregrine stock became worthless. People had told me stocks go up and down, but my first investment had gone down to zero. I lost my savings due to this stupid move. I almost swore off the stock markets forever.

Post Peregrine's closure, I moved to Goldman Sachs. My new colleagues loved to invest in the stock markets too. They would track the US stock markets late at night in Hong Kong, given the time difference. They invested in tech stocks, which were then soaring because of the dotcom boom in the early 2000s. I succumbed and invested again. This time my investments did well, at least for a while. Learning from my past mistake, in order to not be exposed to the fortunes of just one company, I put my money in a diversified tech index fund. Later, I also bought small shares of individual stocks, based on whatever was hot at the time. Some of the companies included DoubleClick (an internet ad company), Tenfold (not sure what they did, but they said software) and eBay. In non-tech, I bought some stocks of FedEx, a courier company. I believed that the rise in e-commerce would mean more parcel deliveries which meant courier companies would do well. FedEx did do well, but the hot tech companies I had bought stocks of soared and then crashed. The dotcom bust came down hard. I suffered more losses. However, this time, most of my money was in the index fund, which is a fund that mirrors the stock market index. A stock market index is an aggregate of several leading companies, and hence it is essentially a diversified portfolio of stocks. My index fund went down in the falling market but didn't fall to zero. My losses mostly meant giving up my profits. My original investment remained safe.

Eventually, I learnt more about stock market investing. I read books, followed Warren Buffet's value-based approach, learnt to research properly and buy the stocks of good companies. I especially liked to invest in companies whose products I liked or used, and whose shares sold at a reasonable price/earnings multiple (a key metric to check if the shares are priced well). I bought shares of

McDonalds, Starbucks and Apple, all brands I personally used. I also invested in real estate in India. I started saving and investing as much as I could right from my first job, which was twenty-five years ago (for example, I invested in Apple around the time the first iPhone was released). Since then, many of my investments have grown manifold.

> ❦ Alongside my job or writing, ESI—earning, saving and investing— has always been a part of my life. ❦

The point of telling you all this is not to show off my investing prowess. I am merely saying that alongside my job or writing, ESI—earning, saving and investing—has always been a part of my life. The only difference between D and me was that my earnings became savings which became investments that grew, while D spent most of his earnings and never saved and invested. This meant that at the age of fifty, D had to find a job as soon as possible to meet his expenses. I, on

> ❦ The markets reward you with luck if you stay in them long-term. ❦

the other hand, didn't have to (and hopefully will never need to) sit in a corporate office again. Is this a luxury? For sure, but I have it because I chose to give up on some other luxuries. Am I lucky? Yes, I am. The markets reward you with luck if you stay in them long-term. Nothing had stopped D from making some of those choices and earning his luck too.

Your Money Mantra: Earn, Save and Invest

The rules you read earlier in the book are meant to help you succeed and win in life. This includes earning more money. However, merely earning money is not enough. Your becoming wealthy depends not only on what you earn, but also on how you save and invest along the way. That's how most ordinary people become wealthy. They earn, save and invest. Does it take a long time? Yes. Does it mean sacrifices are required in life? Yes. Does it mean you are somewhat old by the time you become wealthy? Yes. But at least you get there. You eventually are able to make that class jump and acquire a totally different status if you have a lot of wealth. Sure, you can use it to buy luxury goods like designer clothes, but more importantly, you can use it to make what D rightly calls 'luxurious choices'. Who cares if you have an expensive carpet or painting in your house? What about having the choice to quit your job whenever you want to without worrying about money? That is the ultimate luxury, isn't it?

> Your becoming wealthy depends not only on what you earn, but also on how you save and invest along the way.

Investing

This is not a book on how to become an expert at investing. You will need to read some of those to properly learn about investing. There are dozens of them out there. Some of them are good. I have also made some 'how to invest' videos for the beginner investor. You can look them up on my YouTube channel. The QR code for all my videos on investing is given below.

Here are some basic things to keep in mind for your investment journey:

Step 1: Earning and Saving

The first step in the growing-wealth-by-investing game is to earn. This means you need to get to a point where you have a well-paying job or a profitable business. Only then will you be able to save some of those earnings. To get that job, you need a good degree and/or work experience and/or solid networking. To get a business going takes several years. Meanwhile, try to save at any income level. (I have a YouTube video on exactly that: 'How to save at any income—10K, 20K, 50K, 100K'.) Saving a tiny part of a small income won't make you rich, but it will help you make saving a habit.

Step 2: Investing

Once you have savings, the next step is investing.

Stock markets typically give good returns over time, beat inflation and Fixed Deposits (FD). Stocks are also liquid (which means you can easily sell your investments for cash). You can also invest in index funds or mutual funds (I have videos on these too, in case you want to watch). This lowers the company-specific risk of buying an individual company stock. Systematic Investment Plans, or SIPs, work well for salaried people who want to invest a set amount each month. The downside of stock markets is that they can go down, sometimes by quite a bit. However, in the long term, the odds are likely to be in your favour and you will make money.

Another big investment segment is real estate. This requires larger investments and is more illiquid, which means assets that cannot be easily converted to cash. Typically, you cannot sell property as fast as stocks or bonds. The value of real estate may also go up or down in the short term. Property is expensive and requires large amounts of money. Invest in it only once you have significant savings. And ensure you get good value or a great deal when you buy land or property.

There are other asset classes like gold and precious metals. I don't invest in them because I find their markets hard to understand. Nor do I like crypto, which is extremely sentiment-driven and speculative, relying more on the confidence of people than fundamental business principles. When you buy stocks, you buy an actual percentage share of a company or a number of them. When you buy real estate, you get a house or property. Crypto is not tied to any tangible assets. Even though it may work for some people, it doesn't work for me, and I do not advise it.

Other investments like angel funding, venture cap and private equity are too sophisticated and probably not for the average person. There's a lot of risk and low liquidity in these, though occasionally returns can be massive. Again, I wouldn't advise it for the non-sophisticated investor.

The Dangers of Not Investing

Some people don't like to make risky investments. They earn. They even save. However, they prefer to keep their savings in cash or in FDs. This is the Indian way. Most of our parents and grandparents love FDs. Sure, FDs are better than money in the current account or cash under the pillow. FDs are liquid. They also give you a little bit of interest. However, that interest is taxable and your net return from FDs will often be lower than the rate of inflation, so they make you lose money in the long term. Stocks give much higher returns in the long term. Also, when stocks are sold for profit, a capital gains tax is applicable, which is a lower rate of tax than that of the tax on any income from FDs.

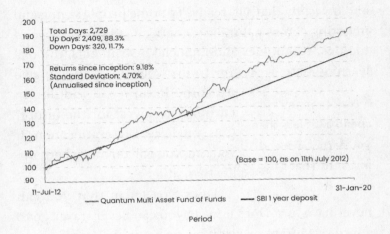

Total Days: 2,729
Up Days: 2,409, 88.3%
Down Days: 320, 11.7%

Returns since inception: 9.18%
Standard Deviation: 4.70%
(Annualised since inception)

(Base = 100, as on 11th July 2012)

11-Jul-12   31-Jan-20

—— Quantum Multi Asset Fund of Funds   —— SBI 1 year deposit

Period

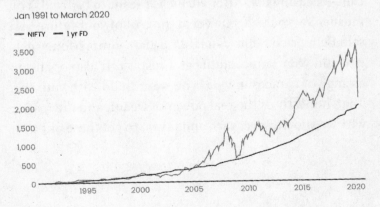

₹10 annual SIP increasing 5% into NIFTY & 1 year FD

Jan 1991 to March 2020

—— NIFTY —— 1 yr FD

GRAPHS SHOWING STOCK MARKET RETURNS VERSUS FIXED DEPOSITS IN BANKS[5]

Final Thoughts on Earning, Saving and Investing

Make money but spend a lot less than you earn. Save and invest it. That's it, really. To some people saving and investing comes naturally. Others must learn it. Beyond the tips, techniques and financial instruments, the real learning here is on how to live your life. Can you give up some luxury you indulge in currently to invest for the future? Can you delay your gratification? If you can, you will do much better in life than others.

❝ Make money but spend a lot less than you earn. Save and invest it. That's it, really. ❞

Does this mean that you can never have fun? Does it mean you can never travel, go to a nice restaurant or just blow up some money shopping for high-priced jeans or an expensive phone? Sure, you can—occasionally. After all, life is meant to be lived. You must enjoy yourself, but not at the cost of your future best self. Being rich helps you make a class jump. Money gets you and your family status and respect. It also opens up a range of choices in what you want to do with your life. That, honestly, is the real power of wealth and the reason why we should save, earn and invest to get there one day.

....

Key Takeaways

■ Make money but spend much less than what you earn. Earn, save and invest.

■ The world may glorify YOLO. Indeed, you only live once! BUT living once also means living and planning for your entire life, not just that moment.

■ Merely earning is not enough. What you have to do is become wealthy and for that you need to practise making smart financial choices and investments.

■ If saving and investing don't come to you naturally, learn about them. Most importantly, you need to learn how to live your life now so that you are investing in your future.

'Earn, save and invest. Makes sense,' Viraj said, 'but long way to go for me. I must earn first.'

'Healthy Burgers' said the label on the packaging of the food I had ordered today. It was from a new place. Can burgers actually be healthy, I wondered.

'That's right, increasing earnings is the first step,' I said.

'And to earn more I must increase my value. Upgrade myself.'

'Exactly. Hopefully the rules will help you.'

I opened my box. The burger had been made with a multigrain bun, which had not been fried. The patty, made of chickpeas, was roasted and not fried either. The burger had no cheese or mayonnaise. I guess it was a healthy dish that resembled a burger. I shut the lid.

'I will miss coming here. Bringing you lunch every day,' Viraj said.

'I will miss you too. You can still come visit. Also, I will still order food.'

'But I won't visit. Nor can I deliver your food.'

'Why?'

'Because I am going to quit,' Viraj said. 'I am going to change my life. I will see you, but only after I have changed my life.'

'Really?'

'Yes. Only after I have made that class jump. Crossed my aukaat.'

'You will.'

'Then I will take you out for lunch ... and I will pay for it,' Viraj said and smiled, determination shining in his eyes.

'Absolutely!'

Viraj stood up. We hugged. He held on to me for several seconds.

'Thank you,' he said after releasing me, his eyes moist, 'I hope I don't let you down ... let myself down.'

'You won't,' I said, looking into his eyes. 'I believe in you.'

'Thank you. That means a lot.' Viraj collected his bag and left.

I looked at my food, the burger robbed of its soul, and wondered what to do with it.

CLOSING NOTE

*'The only person you are destined to become is the
person you decide to be.'*

—RALPH WALDO EMERSON

Thank you for reaching this far in the book. If you read until here, you have something in you. You possess that fire, the desire to live a life that's beyond just the ordinary. You want to make it. You want a better life, and you know you deserve much more. You know you have the capability to do better, but somehow you have faltered from time to time, and could not make it happen. Not anymore. You will now set your mind to it, follow these rules, and make it happen for yourself. You will live a life of purpose, which will be to become the best version of yourself. I can guarantee that you will surprise yourself and others with how far you will reach.

India is not a place where common people can succeed easily. The mighty Iron Gates of the higher classes will block you. Flaming torches of resistance and arrows of humiliation will be thrown at you. Nails and landmines of difficulties will be laid in your path. Chains will be put on you to keep you in your place. Yet, you must pick up your backpack, wear your boots, put on your armour and be ready to climb the dangerous mountain of class.

Is it hard? Yes.

Can you do it? Yes.

Is it worth it? Hell, yes!

Happiness and Fun

As you go about this difficult journey to achieve success in life, I want to remind you not to forget something that is even more important—happiness. Ultimately, all of us seek success in the hope that it will make us happy. There is no point of having all the success in the world if you are not happy.

I am telling you to embark on this long and difficult journey. I am asking you to be disciplined and to work hard on your fitness and career. I want you to build emotional control. Learn English well and develop networking skills. Eat the elephant and be the cockroach. Take accountability and learn to save and invest. There is just so much work to do.

Look at your work positively, whatever it is you do. But don't *only* work. Do take breaks and indulge in fun activities. I am not a military drill sergeant. I am not here to tell you to live a hellish life. I love to have fun. I party, travel, talk nonsense with my close friends and surf the web for pointless things. I even have a drink sometimes and eat all kinds of decadent foods. Life, after all, is meant to be lived. The only thing is, I try to do all this now with awareness and in moderation.

Have fun through this finite life. Even if you have fifty more years to live, that's only 2,500 weekends. Make each one count. Be happy, make others happy. Love yourself, love others. Work hard, relax, enjoy, rest, rinse, repeat. That's it.

If you follow this book, you will have a busy life. However, you will be busy doing things that matter to you and make you better. You will be spending your life aligned with your purpose. When that happens, work won't seem like work. It is difficult to lift weights or to run. Studying late into the night isn't easy either. However, once you attach a positive value to that activity, you will be able to think differently about it. You will go from 'Gosh, I have to do this' to 'Wow, I get to do this'.

This book took time and discipline for me to write. On many days, I sat down to write and felt, 'Oh no, I have to write my daily quota again!' Then, as I started writing, the words started to flow. 'Wow, I get to write this,' I thought. 'It's so amazing I get to write books for a living. It's so great I get to help others.' This book, in particular, helped me talk about things I have never spoken about in the past. Somehow, I felt the reader of this book will be the kind of person that I will be able to trust. And I am grateful I was able to share so many personal things with you. The reason I have shared all that I did is to tell you that I understand what it is like to grow up in tough environments, and if I can do it, you can too.

I am not the only one helping you through this book. You have helped me too, by reading it. I thank you for that. We all have a past and some dark memories. We are all flawed, and the point is really to keep working to get to a better place.

If this book helped you, or if you have anything else you want to share with me, do let me know through my various social media channels listed below. Your journey will inspire others. If you like this book, share what you felt about it on your social media or WhatsApp groups. If you think this book will help others, consider gifting it to them. Help change their lives as well. That will also be the best gift to me, and to books and publishing in general, and the best way to pay it forward.

God bless you all!

FIVE YEARS LATER

We met at Level Up in Gurgaon, a posh and spacious café with leather sofas and brass lamps. It looked more like a five-star hotel lounge than a simple place to have coffee.

'So good to see you,' I said, shaking hands with Viraj.

Viraj was sharply dressed in a dark blue suit and a crisp white shirt. His well-toned arms and flat stomach showed how fit he was. He looked like the younger brother of the Viraj I met five years ago.

He led me to a table.

'Fancy place,' I remarked. 'Nice choice.'

'Thank you,' Viraj said.

Viraj had reached out to me a few weeks ago, after a long gap. He told me he had moved to Gurgaon, and he would love to meet me whenever I was there next. I had come to Delhi for a motivational talk, and we decided to meet after my event.

'You just vanished,' I said. 'Disappeared!'

'I had to. Until I was ready to see you again.'

The waiters brought us two cups of black coffee.

'What have you been up to?' I said, taking a sip.

'I quit Zomato. After that, I met a few restaurant managers for a job. They offered me the position of a waiter. To become a manager, they said I should go to catering school. Do a course in hotel management.'

'Oh.'

'I decided to prepare for the hotel management entrance exam. I did ... cleared IHM Delhi.'

'That's one of the best institutes for hotel management,' I said.

'I prepared day and night.'

'Well done.'

'Thanks. At IHM, I studied hard. Never wasted time on the phone. Quit Instagram. Learnt how to prepare different cuisines, beyond just the course.'

'That's good, Viraj.'

'I also started running and working out in the college gym. Became fit. Academically, I finished college near the top of my class. Developed English skills to do well at interviews. Had offers from Taj and Oberoi to become a management trainee.'

'Amazing. So you work at Taj? Or Oberoi?'

'I worked at Taj for a year. There, I networked with many rich clients who came to the hotel. One of them wanted to invest in a new high-end café. He needed a partner. He would put in the money. The other partner would get equity to run the café.'

'And?'

'The Taj job was good. It paid well and was prestigious. But it was the easier, softer option. I chose my hard, like you'd said. I quit and became the partner. We opened Level Up.'

'Level Up? You mean this place?' I said, spreading my hands to indicate the opulent surroundings.

'I chose this café for us to meet because, well, this is my café.'

I looked at Viraj. He was sitting up straight, confident and proud. My eyes became moist.

'We plan to open three more cafés in Mumbai, Bangalore and Delhi. Seven investors have already expressed interest. I am going to a party at an investor's house tonight.'

'Wow, Viraj,' I said in a soft voice, 'you did it.'

'Still a long way to go, Chetan sir, but I did it. I made that class jump.'

'Yes, you did, and how!'

We stood up and hugged.

'Thank you for putting me on the right path. For helping me rise and level up. That's why it's called Level Up,' Viraj said.

'It was all you,' I said.

He pointed to the entrance of the café. Half a dozen riders from various delivery apps waited on bikes to collect orders.

'See there, Chetan ... all these boys. I was there. Unfit, lonely, sad. Crying for Arpita, the day I came to you. I will never forget where I came from.'

'Do you have love in your life?'

'Right now, I love myself and my work. I'm sure love will find its way into my life eventually. I'll meet plenty of girls at the dinner tonight as well. If only I had the time to date!' he said with a laugh.

'You are a busy man,' I said.

'Yes. Arpita did message though.'

'Oh! How's she doing?'

'Not sure. She wanted to catch up. We are supposed to fix a time to meet and have lunch. But ...' he stopped short of completing the sentence.

'But what?'

'Like I said, I need to find the time. Let's see,' he said.

We looked at each other and smiled.

Viraj and I walked out of the café. He smiled and shook hands with the delivery boys waiting to collect orders.

'Don't just work. Have fun also,' I said as I sat in my car.

'I am. But to be honest, nothing is more fun than getting better,' Viraj said, waving at me as I drove off.

THE END

ACKNOWLEDGEMENTS

How does one write the acknowledgements for a book that took a lifetime of work to write? There are so many people who I met along the way, and in their own way they helped me shape my thoughts, influenced my actions and made me the person I am. Should I thank all of them? Including those who created hardships in my life? Maybe I should, for if I didn't have those people creating obstacles for me, not believing in me, actively trying to harm me, stunting my growth, belittling me and shaming me, I would not have fought back as hard. I won't name those people, as I don't want to stir up things, but they know who they are. Really, thank you! Thank you for making me stronger. Without some of the difficulties that you guys created, I would not have become as resilient and capable. Thank you!

Thanks are, of course, also due to all the positive people in my life, who fortunately greatly outnumber the negative ones. My mother is the prime person, who has kept me going. Even in those rough times as a child, she taught me how to smile and find something good in the terrible world around me. Her belief in me, encouragement for my endeavours and her telling me that it's all going to get better and work out helped me succeed. I could have given up, and to be honest, I did come close to that several times. Then, there would be have been no book titled *11 Rules*. So thank you, Mom!

And then there have been teachers, bankers, publishers, filmmakers, media people, brands, corporate houses, event organizers and, of course, my readers, who have believed in me at various points in my life and continue to do so. Thank you to all of you! There are so many of you I am grateful for that I would need an entire book to cover all your names. But without your support, nothing would have happened for me. And if I did nothing in my life, where would I have got the experiences on which I have based this book?

There are also those who helped me specifically with this book. These include:

Shinie Antony, my editor and friend for nearly two decades. Her guidance and support are invaluable.

The group of early readers who gave wonderful feedback on the manuscript: Bhakti Bhat, Ishaan Bhagat, Jatin Jain, Nimisha Elizabeth Dean, Shyam Bhagat, Venessa Fernandes and Virali Jain. Thank you all for your help and suggestions for the book.

The editors at HarperCollins India. The entire marketing, sales, social media and production teams at HarperCollins India as well. To all the online delivery boys and girls who help with the delivery of books to every nook and corner of the country. To the salespersons in bookshops and the airport and train station kiosks.

To all those who follow me on social media—Facebook, Instagram, Twitter, Threads and YouTube. I am thankful to all of you. Especially to those who give me feedback on my motivational talks and videos, which in turn helped me make this book better.

My family—a pillar of support in my life. My mother, Rekha Bhagat, my wife, Anusha, and my children, Shyam and Ishaan. My brother, Ketan, and nephew, Rian. My in-laws, Suryanarayan Annaswamy and Kalpana Suryanarayan. My brother-in-law, Anand, my sister-in-law, Poornima, and their children, Ananya and Karan. Thank you all for being there.

REFERENCES

1. Huberman Lab Podcast: https://www.youtube.com/watch?v=h2aWYjSA1Jc

2. Joseph Troncale, 'Your Lizard Brain: The Limbic System and Brain Functioning', Psychology Today, 22 April 2014, https://www.psychologytoday.com/us/blog/where-addiction-meets-your-brain/201404/your-lizard-brain

3. Anna Lembke, *Dopamine Nation: Finding Balance in the Age of Indulgence*, Dutton, 2021.

4. Daniel Z. Lieberman and Michael E. Long, *The Molecule of More: How a Single Chemical in Your Brain Drives Love, Sex, and Creativity—and Will Determine the Fate of the Human Race*, BenBella Books, 2019.

5. Data sources: www.sbi.co.in, www.nseindia.com, www.amfiindia.com, and www.equitymaster.com

DISCLAIMER

This book is primarily a work of non-fiction. However, it should be noted that certain sections incorporate fictionalized scenarios involving real-world places, companies and brands. These instances of fiction have been included to provide a more engaging and relatable narrative, utilizing names and brands that are commonly recognized in contemporary discourse. The use of real names and locations in these fictional scenarios is for narrative purposes only and should not be interpreted as factual representations. The author in no way represents any company, corporation, or brand mentioned herein. All brands mentioned in the book are owned by their respective owners.

The character of Viraj Shukla and all the conversations with him depicted in this book are entirely fictional. Any resemblance to actual persons, living or dead, or actual events is purely coincidental. The dialogue, characters and situations presented within these pages are products of the author's imagination and are not intended to represent actual events or individuals. Some names and identifying details have been changed to protect the privacy of the individuals in this book. The assertions made and the views and opinions expressed in this book are the author's own and the facts are as reported by him. The publishers are in no way liable for the same. Some of the dialogues contained herein have been created and/or supplemented, some of the events contained herein have been compressed and/or embellished, and the facts are as reported by him. The publishers are in no way liable for the same. Any liability arising from any action undertaken by any person by relying upon any part of this book is strictly disclaimed.

ABOUT THE AUTHOR

Chetan Bhagat is the author of thirteen blockbuster books. These include ten novels—*Five Point Someone, One Night @ the Call Center, The 3 Mistakes of My Life, 2 States, Revolution 2020, Half Girlfriend, One Indian Girl, The Girl in Room 105, One Arranged Murder, 400 Days*—and three non-fiction titles—*What Young India Wants, Making India Awesome* and *India Positive*. Chetan's books have remained bestsellers since their release. Many of his novels have been adapted into successful Bollywood films such as *3 Idiots, 2 States* and *Kai Po Che!*

The New York Times called him the 'the biggest selling English language novelist in India's history'. *Time* magazine recognized him amongst the '100 most influential people in the world' while Fast Company, USA, listed him as one of the world's '100 most creative people in business'. Chetan writes columns for leading English and Hindi newspapers, focusing on youth and national development issues. He is also a motivational speaker, screenplay writer, YouTuber and podcaster.

Chetan quit his international investment banking career in 2009 to dedicate his time entirely to writing and driving positive change in the country.

Chetan studied at IIT-Delhi and IIM-Ahmedabad. He is married to Anusha, an ex-classmate from IIM-A, and they have twin boys, Shyam and Ishaan.

Get in touch with Chetan Bhagat and access content created by him here:

Instagram

X

Facebook

YouTube

Threads

LinkedIn

Spotify

Moj

Website

HarperCollins *Publishers* India

At HarperCollins India, we believe in telling the best stories and finding the widest readership for our books in every format possible. We started publishing in 1992; a great deal has changed since then, but what has remained constant is the passion with which our authors write their books, the love with which readers receive them, and the sheer joy and excitement that we as publishers feel in being a part of the publishing process.

Over the years, we've had the pleasure of publishing some of the finest writing from the subcontinent and around the world, including several award-winning titles and some of the biggest bestsellers in India's publishing history. But nothing has meant more to us than the fact that millions of people have read the books we published, and that somewhere, a book of ours might have made a difference.

As we look to the future, we go back to that one word—a word which has been a driving force for us all these years.

Read.

Harper Collins

HARPER PERENNIAL

HARPER BUSINESS

HARPER BLACK

हार्पर हिन्दी

HarperCollins *Children's Books*

HARPER DESIGN

HARPER VANTAGE

Harper Sport